U.S. Immigration
and Migration
Biographies

U.S. Immigration and Migration
Biographies

Volume 2
K–Z

James L. Outman,
Roger Matuz, and
Rebecca Valentine

Lawrence W. Baker,
Project Editor

Detroit • New York • San Diego • San Francisco • Cleveland • New Haven, Conn. • Waterville, Maine • London • Munich

U.S. Immigration and Migration: Biographies

James L. Outman, Roger Matuz, Rebecca Valentine

Project Editor
Lawrence W. Baker

Editorial
Sarah Hermsen, Diane Sawinski

Permissions
Lori Hines

Imaging and Multimedia
Dean Dauphinais, Lezlie Light,
Mike Logusz

Product Design
Pamela A. E. Galbreath, Kate Scheible

Composition
Evi Seoud

Manufacturing
Rita Wimberley

LIBRARY OF CONGRESS CATALOGING-IN-PUBLICATION DATA

Outman, James L., 1946–

U.S. immigration and migration. Biographies / James L. Outman, Roger Matuz, Rebecca Valentine ; Lawrence W. Baker, editor.

p. cm. — ([U.S. immigration and migration reference library])

Includes bibliographical references and index.

ISBN 0-7876-7733-7 (set : hardcover : alk. paper) — ISBN 0-7876-7568-7 (v. 1) — ISBN 0-7876-7668-3 (v. 2)

1. United States—Emigration and immigration—Juvenile literature. 2. United States—Emigration and immigration—Government policy—Juvenile literature. 3. Immigrants—United States—Biography—Juvenile literature. 4. Immigration advocates—United States—Biography—Juvenile literature. 5. Immigration opponents—United States—Biography—Juvenile literature. I. Title: US immigration and migration. Biographies. II. Matuz, Roger. III. Valentine, Rebecca. IV. Baker, Lawrence W. V. Title. VI. Series.

JV6465.O88 2004
304.8'73'0922—dc22
2004003552

Printed in the United States of America
10 9 8 7 6 5 4 3 2

Contents

Reader's Guide

The U.S. Constitution, signed in 1789, gave Congress the right to create laws involving immigration and citizenship. When the first Congress assembled, it created a loose idea of what it meant to be a citizen of the United States: all "free white persons" who had lived in the country for a couple of years were eligible. But the concept of citizenship was still vague. The naturalization process—the set of rules for becoming a citizen—was initially quite simple. The young nation actively sought immigrants to bring their professional skills and labor and to take part in expanding the borders of the nation from the Atlantic Ocean to the Pacific Ocean. There were initially no immigration agencies or border patrols—no passports or green cards. But not everyone was allowed to become a citizen or afforded the same rights. Issues of race for non-whites and Hispanics as well as a historical preference for the northwestern European immigrants led to inequalities and discrimination from the start.

Legislations and policies have continually added to or changed the original vague requirements, rights, and responsibilities of citizenship and immigration. Through the Fourteenth and Fifteenth Amendments after the American Civil War (1861–65), the concept of the "free white persons" eligible to become citizens was amended to include African Americans. Women's citizenship generally was dependent on their husband or father's citizenship until 1920. Until 1943, most Asians were not included in the definition of someone who could become a citizen.

American sentiment toward immigrants has always gone back and forth between positive and negative for a number of reasons. During good economic times when labor is needed, immigrants usually receive better treatment than during economic downturns when people fear the competition for employment. When mass migrations from particular areas begin, there is often hostility in the United States toward the latest group to arrive. They are often perceived as different and as a threat to "American values," leaning more toward Western European traditions. Immigration has almost always been at the center of political controversy in the United States. In fact, the first anti-immigrant government policies began to arise within only a few years of the signing of the Constitution.

Immigration restrictions brought about by nativist (favoring the interests of people who are native-born to a country, though generally not concerning Native Americans, as opposed to its immigrants), racist, or anti-immigrant attitudes have had a very major impact on the U.S. population, dictating who entered the country and in what numbers. The Chinese, for example, were virtually stopped from immigrating by the Chinese Exclusion Act of 1882 until it was repealed in 1943. Many families were separated for decades because of the severity of U.S. restrictions. Immigration from many other countries was significantly reduced by the immigration quota (assigned proportions) systems of 1921 and 1924.

Most immigrants, since the first English settlers landed at Jamestown, have had to pay tremendous dues to settle in North America. There has been a long-held pattern in which the latest arrivals have often been forced to take on the lowest-paying and most undesirable jobs. However, many historians of immigration point out that the brightest and most promising professional prospects of the nations of the world have immigrated to the United States. A daring spirit and the ability to overcome obstacles have always been, and continue to be today, qualities common to the immigrants coming into the nation.

The United States differs from many other countries of the world in having a population made up of people descended from all of the world's nations. Immigration controversy continues to confront the United States in the early twenty-first century, posing difficult questions from concerns about regulating entry and controlling undocumented immigration, to providing public services and a decent education to recently arrived immigrants. In the early years of the twenty-first century, the U.S. Marines intercepted refugees from the civil uprising in Haiti and sent them back to their country, where they feared for their lives. When does the United States provide refuge and what makes the nation deny others who are in need? These concerns are not likely to be resolved in the near future. The value of studying the historical and cultural background of immigration and migration in the nation goes well beyond understanding these difficult issues.

Why study immigration and migration?

As a chronicle of the American people's roots, the history of immigration and migration provides a very intimate approach to the nation's past. Immigration history is strongly centered on the people of the United States rather than the presidential administrations or the wars the nation has fought. Learning about the waves of immigration and migration that populated the continent and seeing the American culture as the mix of many cultures is central to understanding the rich diversity of the United States and appreciating it as a multicultural nation.

The two-volume *U.S. Immigration and Migration: Biographies* presents the life stories of fifty individuals who either played key roles in the governmental and societal influences on U.S. immigration and migration or are immigrants who became successful in the United States. Profiled are well-known figures such as German-born physicist Albert Einstein; Scottish-born industrialist Andrew Carnegie; Czech-born Madeleine Albright, the first female U.S. secretary of state; and English-born comedic actor Charlie Chaplin. In addition, lesser-known individuals are featured, such as Kalpana Chawla, the first female astronaut from India; Mexican-born Antonia Hernández, a lawyer and activist for Latino causes; and folk singer Woody Guthrie, whose songs focused on the plight of victims of the Great Depression and the Dust Bowl of the 1930s—migrants who left the Midwest in search of a better life in the West.

U.S. Immigration and Migration: Biographies also features sidebars containing interesting facts about people and events related to immigration and migration. Within each full-length biography, boldfaced cross-references direct readers to other individuals profiled in the set. Finally, each volume includes photographs and illustrations, a "U.S. Immigration and Migration Timeline" that lists significant dates and events related to immigration and migration as well as the biographees, and an index.

U.S. Immigration and Migration Reference Library

U.S. Immigration and Migration: Biographies is only one component of the three-part U.S. Immigration and Migration Reference Library. The other two titles in this set are:

- *U.S. Immigration and Migration: Almanac* (two volumes) presents a comprehensive overview of the groups of people who have immigrated to the United States from the nations of Africa, Europe, Asia, and Latin America, as well as those who migrated within the country to unexplored lands or to newly industrialized cities. Its seventeen chapters include information on groups or clusters of groups of immigrants from other nations and cultures: Pre-Columbian; Spanish; English; Scotch and Scotch-Irish; French and Dutch; Africans; German; Irish; Scandinavian; Chinese, Japanese, and Filipino; Jewish; Italian and Greek; Eastern European; Arab; Asian Indian, Korean, and Southeast Asian; Mexican; and other Latino and Caribbean groups. Internal migration is also covered, including westward expansion, forced migration, and industrialization and urbanization. The *Almanac* also contains more than 150 black-and-white photographs and maps, "Fact Focus" and "Words to Know" boxes, a "Research and Activity Ideas" section, a timeline, and an index.

- *U.S. Immigration and Migration: Primary Sources:* This volume tells the story of U.S. immigration and migration in the words of the people who lived and shaped it. Eighteen excerpted documents provide a wide range of perspectives on this period of history. Included are excerpts from presidential vetoes; judicial rulings; various legislative acts and treaties; personal essays; magazine articles; party platforms; and works of fiction featuring immigrants.

- A cumulative index of all three titles in the U.S. Immigration and Migration Reference Library is also available.

Acknowledgments

Thanks to copyeditor Theresa Murray; proofreader Amy Marcaccio Keyzer; the indexers from Synapse, the Knowledge Link Corporation; and typesetter Jake Di Vita of the Graphix Group for their fine work. Additional thanks to Julie Burwinkel, media director at Ursuline Academy, Cincinnati, Ohio, and Janet Sarratt, library media specialist at John E. Ewing Middle School, Gaffney, South Carolina, for their help during the early stages of the project.

Comments and suggestions

We welcome your comments on *U.S. Immigration and Migration: Biographies* as well as your suggestions for topics to be featured in future editions. Please write to: Editor, *U.S. Immigration and Migration: Biographies,* U•X•L, 27500 Drake Road, Farmington Hills, Michigan, 48331-3535; call toll-free: 800-877-4253; fax to 248-414-5043; or send e-mail via http://www.gale.com.

U.S. Immigration and Migration Timeline

c. 13,000 B.C.E. The first immigrants arrive on the North American continent and gradually migrate in groups throughout North and South America. Neither the timing of the first migrations nor their origins are known.

c. 400 C.E. The Anasazi culture emerges in the Four Corners region of present-day Arizona, New Mexico, Utah, and Colorado. The Anasazi, thought to be the ancestors of the Pueblo, Zuni, and Hopi Indians, were known for their basketry and pottery as well as their elaborate mansions built into high cliff walls.

c. 700 People of the moundbuilding Mississippian culture build the city of Cahokia near present-day East St.

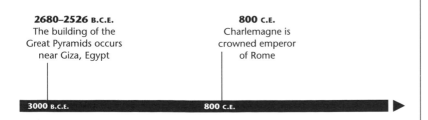

2680–2526 B.C.E.
The building of the Great Pyramids occurs near Giza, Egypt

800 C.E.
Charlemagne is crowned emperor of Rome

3000 B.C.E.   **800** C.E.

Louis, Illinois, about five square miles wide, and containing about a hundred mounds situated around central plazas.

1000   Norse explorer Leif Eriksson sets out from Greenland and apparently sails to Vinland, in present-day Newfoundland, Canada.

1492   Navigator Christopher Columbus arrives in the Caribbean while searching for a route to Asia on an expedition for the kingdom of Spain. He returns to Hispaniola (the island which today is home to Haiti and the Dominican Republic) with settlers the following year.

1565   Spanish explorers and settlers establish Saint Augustine, Florida, the oldest permanent European settlement in the United States.

1607   The Jamestown settlers from England arrive in Virginia and establish a colony.

1618–1725   From five to seven thousand Huguenots flee the persecution in France and sail to America to settle in the British colonies.

1619   A Dutch warship brings twenty African slaves to Jamestown, Virginia, the first Africans to arrive in the British colonies.

1620   The Pilgrims and other British colonists aboard the *Mayflower* land in Plymouth Harbor to found a new British colony.

1624   The first wave of Dutch immigrants to New Netherlands arrives in what is now New York. Most settle at Fort Orange, where the city of Albany now stands.

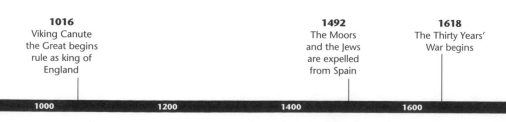

1016
Viking Canute
the Great begins
rule as king of
England

1492
The Moors
and the Jews
are expelled
from Spain

1618
The Thirty Years'
War begins

1000   1200   1400   1600

1630–40 In the Great Migration from England to New England, about twenty thousand men, women, and children, many of them Puritans, migrate.

1649 An Act Concerning Religion (The Maryland Toleration Act) is issued, allowing the English colony of Maryland to be a refuge for English Catholics who were often persecuted for their beliefs during the English civil war. The act sets the stage for future religious freedoms.

1718 The vast territory of Louisiana becomes a province of France; the European population of the colony numbers about four hundred.

1769 Two Spanish expeditions—one by land and one by sea—leave Mexico to colonize Alta California, the present-day state of California.

1774 English-born scientist **Joseph Priestley** discovers oxygen. Twenty years later, he leaves for America with his family, and soon thereafter establishes the first Unitarian Church in Philadelphia, Pennsylvania.

1784 The Treaty of Fort Stanwix is enacted; the United States agrees to give Native Americans control of the western territory in an attempt to protect native lands from further takeovers by Europeans. However, European settlers ignore the act and it is never enforced by either the British or the U.S. government.

1789 English immigrant **Samuel Slater** brings secret designs of early textile machinery to the United States. He later builds a textile mill in Pawtucket, Rhode Island, the first of many that Slater will own and operate in New England.

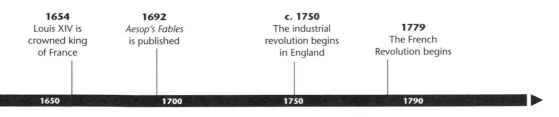

1654
Louis XIV is
crowned king
of France

1692
Aesop's Fables
is published

c. 1750
The industrial
revolution begins
in England

1779
The French
Revolution begins

1650   1700   1750   1790

1790 Congress passes an act providing that "free white persons" who have lived in the United States for at least two years can be naturalized (become citizens) in any U.S. court. Along with non-white males, this also excludes indentured servants, slaves, children, and most women, all of whom are considered dependents.

1804 Meriwether Lewis and William Clark set out on their overland trip across the continent to the Pacific Ocean, forging a path never before explored by European Americans.

1808 Congress prohibits the importation of slaves into the United States, but the slave trade continues until the end of the American Civil War in 1865.

1808 German immigrant **John Jacob Astor** organizes the American Fur Company in Oregon.

1815–45 About one million Irish Catholics immigrate to the United States.

1825 A group of Norwegians immigrate to the United States, eventually settling in Illinois, where they begin the Fox River settlement. This serves as the base camp for future Norwegian immigrants to the United States.

1827 Haitian-born **John James Audubon** publishes the first volume of his *Birds in America* series of illustrations.

1830s Many tribes from the Northeast and Southeast are forcibly moved to Indian Territory (present-day Oklahoma and Kansas). Southern tribes to be removed include the Cherokee, Chickasaw, Choctaw, Creek, Seminole, and others. In the North, the Delaware, Miami, Ottawa, Peoria, Potawatomi, Sauk and Fox, Seneca, and Wyandot tribes are removed. The government is not prepared to provide supplies for so many

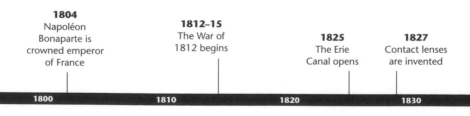

1804
Napoléon Bonaparte is crowned emperor of France

1812–15
The War of 1812 begins

1825
The Erie Canal opens

1827
Contact lenses are invented

1800   1810   1820   1830

Indians along the trails and in new homes, causing great suffering and death for the Native Americans.

1830s The mass migration of Germans to the United States begins.

1835 French immigrant **Alexis de Tocqueville**'s book *On Democracy in America* is first published, becoming a best-seller. It will remain a unique study of everyday American society during a period of rapid growth marked by a steady immigration of Europeans to the United States.

1836 The Mexican province of Texas declares its independence from Mexico. Texas will become a state in 1845.

1836–60 The Jewish population of the United States grows from fewer than 15,000 to about 160,000. Most of the Jewish immigrants during this period are from Germany.

1841 The first wagon trains cross the continent on the Oregon Trail.

1845 The potato crop in Ireland is hit with a mysterious disease, beginning the Irish potato famine. By the winter of 1847, tens of thousands of people are dying of starvation or related diseases. An estimated one to one and a half million Irish Catholics leave Ireland for the United States over the next few years.

1846 Swiss naturalist **Louis Agassiz** arrives in Boston, Massachusetts, to great acclaim; he will become a professor at Harvard University, bringing his enthusiasm for natural-history research to American students.

1848 Thirteen-year-old **Andrew Carnegie** and his family leave Germany for the United States. He will grow up

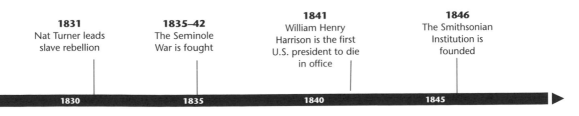

1831
Nat Turner leads
slave rebellion

1835–42
The Seminole
War is fought

1841
William Henry
Harrison is the first
U.S. president to die
in office

1846
The Smithsonian
Institution is
founded

1830   1835   1840   1845

to be one of the most successful immigrants to ever come to America.

1848   After the Mexican-American War, the United States acquires the Mexican provinces of New Mexico, Arizona, California, and parts of Nevada, Colorado, and Utah. Between 80,000 and 100,000 Mexicans suddenly find themselves living in the United States. Those who choose to stay in their homes automatically become citizens of the United States.

1848   Gold is discovered in the foothills of northern California's Sierra Nevada Mountains. In the next few years, hundreds of thousands of people from all over the United States and around the world migrate to California hoping to strike it rich.

1848–1914   An estimated 400,000 Czechs immigrate to the United States from Austria-Hungary.

1850   **Millard Fillmore** becomes U.S. president after the sudden death of Zachary Taylor. Fillmore, known for his anti-immigrant prejudice, will suffer an overwhelming loss in the presidential election of 1856.

1850s   Having escaped slavery, **Harriet Tubman** becomes a "conductor" on the Underground Railroad, a secret network of houses where escaping slaves could safely be hidden on their way to Canada.

1850s   Anti-immigrant associations, such as the American Party (also known as the Know-Nothing Party), the Order of United Americans, and the Order of the Star-Spangled Banner, are on the rise. Their primary targets are Catholics, primarily Irish Americans and German Americans.

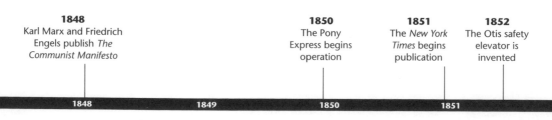

1848
Karl Marx and Friedrich Engels publish *The Communist Manifesto*

1850
The Pony Express begins operation

1851
The *New York Times* begins publication

1852
The Otis safety elevator is invented

1848   1849   1850   1851

1851–1929 More than 1.2 million Swedish immigrants enter the United States.

1855 Castle Island, operated by the State of New York, becomes the first central immigrant-processing center in the United States.

1855 The anti-immigration Know-Nothing Party reveals its platform. A year later, former president Millard Fillmore is this party's candidate in the presidential election; he loses.

1862 Congress passes the Homestead Act to encourage people to settle west of the Mississippi River. Under this act, a person can gain ownership of 160 acres simply by living on the land and cultivating it for five years.

1864–69 Thousands of Chinese laborers work on the first transcontinental railroad in the United States, cutting a path through treacherous mountains.

1866–1914 More than 600,000 Norwegians immigrate to the United States.

1867–1914 About 1.8 Hungarians immigrate to the United States.

1868 The Fourteenth Amendment of the Constitution provides citizenship rights to African Americans.

1869 The first transcontinental railroad in the United States is completed.

1869 German-born engineer and bridge designer **John Augustus Roebling** dies, never seeing his famous Brooklyn Bridge completed.

1870 The Fifteenth Amendment gives African American citizens the right to vote.

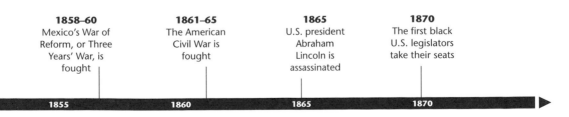

1858–60	**1861–65**	**1865**	**1870**
Mexico's War of Reform, or Three Years' War, is fought	The American Civil War is fought	U.S. president Abraham Lincoln is assassinated	The first black U.S. legislators take their seats

| 1855 | 1860 | 1865 | 1870 |

1870 Polish serfs are given their freedom and begin to emigrate. Up to two million Poles will immigrate to the United States between 1870 and 1914.

1870–1920 About 340,000 Finns immigrate to the United States.

1872 Hungarian immigrant **Joseph Pulitzer** buys the struggling *St. Louis Post,* which begins his career as a newspaper publisher.

1874 As a member of the Knights of Labor, Irish immigrant **Mary Jones** travels to Pennsylvania to provide support for the coal miners who had been on strike for over a year. During this time, Jones earns the nickname "Mother Jones" for her ability to boost the morale of her fellow strikers.

1876 Scottish native **Alexander Graham Bell** receives a patent for an "electric speaking telephone," thought to be the most valuable single patent ever granted.

1877 At Bear Paw, Montana, Colonel Nelson Miles leads an assault on the Nez Perce tribe. **Chief Joseph** tries to negotiate a peaceful end to the suffering endured by his people, who had been driven from their tribal homeland.

1880–1920 About 35 million people, mainly from southern and eastern Europe, arrive on U.S. shores.

1880–1920 About 4 million people leave Italy for the United States, making Italians the single largest European national group of this era of mass migration to move to America.

1880–1924 About 95,000 Arabs immigrate to the United States, most from the area known as Greater Syria—present-day Syria, Lebanon, Jordan, Palestine, and Israel.

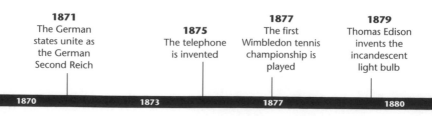

1871
The German states unite as the German Second Reich

1875
The telephone is invented

1877
The first Wimbledon tennis championship is played

1879
Thomas Edison invents the incandescent light bulb

1870   1873   1877   1880

1881–1914 About 2 million Eastern European Jews arrive in the United States.

1882 The Chinese Exclusion Act prohibits the naturalization of Chinese immigrants for ten years and prohibits Chinese laborers from entering the country. For the Chinese already in the country, it denies hope of gaining citizenship and for many Chinese men it meant that their wives or families would not be able to join them. The act, the first major restriction on immigration in the United States, is extended twice and becomes permanent in 1902.

1884 **Helen Hunt Jackson** finishes *Ramona,* her novel inspired by the struggles of Native Americans who are enduring oppression and forced relocation by the U.S. government.

1885–1924 About 200,000 Japanese people immigrate to Hawaii.

1886 More than a million people turn out to see the **Statue of Liberty** unveiled. Designed by French sculptor Frédéric Auguste Bartholdi, the torch-bearing statue becomes a symbol of American freedom.

1889 **Jane Addams** and a traveling companion, teacher Ellen Gates Starr, found Hull House, a community and social center dedicated to helping the working poor and immigrants in Chicago, Illinois, during the time of American industrialization.

1890 Canadian-born businessman **James J. Hill** reorganizes his railroad building company as the Great Northern Railway Company. The company lays tracks connecting Minnesota to Washington State, opening up the Pacific Northwest to settlers and railroad workers who

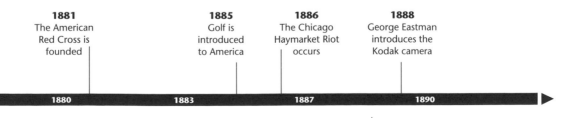

1881
The American Red Cross is founded

1885
Golf is introduced to America

1886
The Chicago Haymarket Riot occurs

1888
George Eastman introduces the Kodak camera

1880   1883   1887   1890

were willing to establish their farms and homes along the railroad's path.

1890   The Superintendent of the United States Census issues a statement that the American frontier has closed—that is, it has become populated and is therefore no longer a frontier.

1891   The Immigration and Naturalization Service (INS) is created as the department that administers federal laws relating to admitting, excluding, or deporting aliens and to naturalizing the foreign-born who are in the United States legally. It remains in operation until 2003.

1892   The federal government takes over the process of screening incoming immigrants at the Port of New York and creates an immigration reception center at Ellis Island, one mile southwest of Manhattan. Before it closes in 1954, more than 16 million immigrants will pass through Ellis Island.

1900   In this one year, one-tenth of Denmark's total population immigrates to the United States.

1903   The last five lines of the poem "The New Colossus" are engraved on a plaque and affixed to the Statue of Liberty. **Emma Lazarus**, the poem's author and an advocate of Jewish rights, had died in 1887 and did not live to see her work displayed on the statue.

1905   German-born **Albert Einstein** publishes a series of papers, including one based on a concept known as Einstein's "special theory of relativity."

1907   The Dillingham Commission, set up by Congress to investigate immigration, produces a forty-two-volume report. The commission claims that its studies show that people from southern and eastern Europe have a

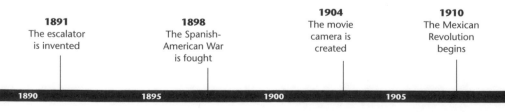

1891
The escalator is invented

1898
The Spanish-American War is fought

1904
The movie camera is created

1910
The Mexican Revolution begins

1890   1895   1900   1905

higher potential for criminal activity, are more likely to end up poor and sick, and are less intelligent than other Americans. The report warns that the waves of immigration threaten the "American" way of life.

1907 As anti-Asian immigrant sentiment rises in the United States, Congress works out the "Gentlemen's Agreement" with Japan, in which the United States agrees not to ban all Japanese immigration as long as Japan promises not to issue passports to Japanese laborers for travel to the continental United States.

1910 To enforce the Chinese Exclusion Act, an immigration station is built at Angel Island in the San Francisco Bay. Any Chinese people arriving in San Francisco go through an initial inspection upon arrival; many are then sent to Angel Island for further processing and thousands are held there for long periods of time.

1910–1920 Between 500,000 and 1,000,000 African Americans migrate from the southern United States to the cities of the North.

1912 Jane Addams publishes *Twenty Years at Hull-House,* in which she writes of her experiences as owner of a house primarily designed to help immigrants trying to adjust to a completely different way of life.

1913 California passes the Alien Land Laws, which prohibit Chinese and Japanese people from owning land in the state.

1914 Swiss-born silent movie star **Charlie Chaplin** appears in his first production, *Kid Auto Races at Venice.*

1917 Congress creates the "Asiatic barred zone," which excludes immigration from most of Asia, including China, India, and Japan, regardless of literacy.

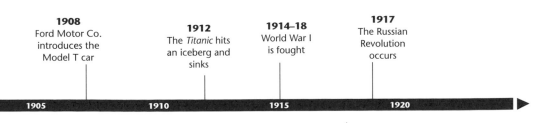

1908
Ford Motor Co. introduces the Model T car

1912
The *Titanic* hits an iceberg and sinks

1914–18
World War I is fought

1917
The Russian Revolution occurs

1905   1910   1915   1920

1920 Jamaican-born **Marcus Garvey** organizes the first of several international conventions, adopting a document titled the "Declaration of Rights of the Negro People of the World." It is a concise statement of Garvey's philosophy of black pride, unity, and immigration to Africa.

1920s–30s More than 40,000 Russians come to the United States in the first few years after the Russian Revolution of 1917. Many Russians go into exile in other European cities. In the 1930s, those in exile in Europe begin fleeing the rising Nazi movement. More than a million people who had been born in Russia but were living elsewhere in Europe immigrate to the United States in the 1930s.

1921 Congress passes the Emergency Quota Act, which stipulates that each nation has an annual quota (proportion) of immigrants it may send to the United States, which is equal to 3 percent of that country's total population in the United States in 1910. Because the majority of the U.S. population was from northwestern Europe in 1910, this method favors northwestern Europeans over other immigrants.

1921 In *Ozawa v. United States,* the U.S. Supreme Court rules against an upstanding twenty-year Chinese immigrant resident of the United States who had applied to become a U.S. citizen on the grounds that he was not "white."

1924 Congress passes the Immigration Act of 1924 (National Origins Act), which restricts the number of immigrants even beyond the Emergency Quota Act of 1921. Under the new act, immigration is decreased to a total equaling 2 percent of the population in 1890. Under

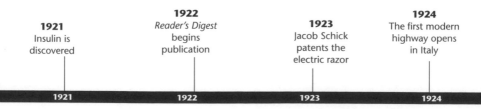

1921
Insulin is
discovered

1922
Reader's Digest
begins
publication

1923
Jacob Schick
patents the
electric razor

1924
The first modern
highway opens
in Italy

1921   1922   1923   1924

this act, each country may only send 2 percent of its 1890 population in the United States per year. The new act skews the permitted immigration even further in favor of Western Europe, with the United Kingdom, Germany, and Ireland receiving more than two-thirds of the annual maximum quota. This legislation ends the era of mass migrations to the United States.

1924   The Oriental Exclusion Act prohibits most Asian immigration, including the wives and children of U.S. citizens of Chinese ancestry.

1924   Congress creates the Border Patrol, a uniformed law enforcement agency of the Immigration Bureau in charge of fighting smuggling and illegal immigration.

1925   One out of every four Greek men between the ages of fifteen and forty-five have immigrated to the United States.

1927   The first of a trilogy of novels by Norwegian-born writer **O. E. Rölvaag** is published. The writings chronicle the lives of immigrants in Minnesota and South Dakota.

1927   Lithuanian native **Al Jolson** stars in the role of Jack Robin in the first successful sound movie, *The Jazz Singer.*

1928   The Notre Dame football team defeats Army, 12-6. Before the game, Notre Dame's coach, Norwegian immigrant **Knute Rockne**, gives his famous locker-room speech that includes the phrase, "Win one for the Gipper."

1931   Hungarian immigrant **Bela Lugosi** plays the leading role in the Universal Studios film *Dracula,* the first talking horror movie.

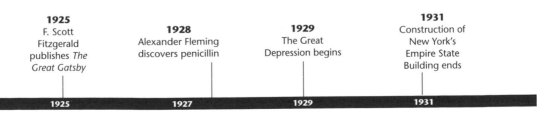

1925
F. Scott Fitzgerald publishes *The Great Gatsby*

1928
Alexander Fleming discovers penicillin

1929
The Great Depression begins

1931
Construction of New York's Empire State Building ends

1925   1927   1929   1931

1934 The Tydings-McDuffie Act sets the date and some of the terms of independence for the Philippines on July 4, 1946. Since the United States had acquired the Philippines from Spain in 1898, Filipinos had entered the United States as nationals (people who live in a country legally, are loyal to the country and protected by it, but are not citizens). The act takes away status of Filipinos as U.S. nationals, reclassifying them as aliens, and restricts Filipino immigration by establishing an annual immigration quota of 50.

Late 1930s **Woody Guthrie** begins his career as a folk singer, known primarily for providing a voice for those displaced by the Great Depression and the Great Dust Storm.

1938 Italian native **Enrico Fermi** receives the Nobel Prize in physics. The Fermi family travels to Sweden, attends the ceremonies, then boards a ship to the United States.

1938 **Henry Kissinger** comes to the United States as a child refugee from Nazi Germany.

1939 U.S. president Franklin D. Roosevelt appoints Austrian native **Felix Frankfurter** to the U.S. Supreme Court. The Senate unanimously confirms the decision to appoint Frankfurter, who, as a boy, had immigrated to New York with his family to escape Austria's persecution of its Jewish inhabitants.

1941 A top-secret study on nuclear fission, called the Manhattan Project, is established in 1941. Enrico Fermi is one of those working on the project.

1942 The United States, heavily involved in World War II, needs laborers at home and turns to Mexico. The U.S. and Mexican governments reach an agreement called

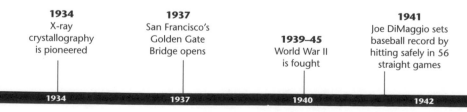

1934
X-ray crystallography is pioneered

1937
San Francisco's Golden Gate Bridge opens

1939–45
World War II is fought

1941
Joe DiMaggio sets baseball record by hitting safely in 56 straight games

1934   1937   1940   1942

the Mexican Farm Labor Supply Program, or the *bracero* program. The program permits Mexicans to enter the country to work under contract as farm and railroad laborers. The program continues for twenty-two years and brings 4.8 million Mexicans to work on U.S. farms and in businesses.

1942   During World War II, President Franklin D. Roosevelt signs Executive Order 9066, which dictates the removal and internment of Japanese Americans. More than 112,000 Japanese Americans living along the Pacific coast are taken from their homes and placed in ten internment camps for the duration of the war.

1943   Congress repeals the Chinese exclusion acts. Immigration from China resumes. Most of the new immigrants are females, the wives of Chinese men who have been in the United States for decades.

1945   As World War II ends, more than 40,000 refugees from Europe flee to the United States. Because the quota system does not provide for them, they are admitted under presidential directive.

1945   The War Brides Act allows foreign-born spouses and adopted children of personnel of the U.S. armed forces to enter the United States. The act brings in many Japanese, Chinese, and Korean women, among other groups.

1948   The first U.S. refugee policy, the Displaced Persons Act, enables nearly 410,000 European refugees to enter the United States after World War II.

1950   The Internal Security Act forces all communists to register with the government and denies admission to any foreigner who is a communist or who might engage in subversive activities.

1945
George Orwell publishes *Animal Farm*

1946
The Cold War between the United States and the Soviet Union begins

1947
Jackie Robinson becomes the first black major league baseball player

1950
The Korean War begins

1944   1946   1948   1950

1951 Chinese immigrant **An Wang** founds Wang Laboratories to develop, produce, and market applications using his memory cores and other inventions.

1952 Congress overrides President Harry S. Truman's veto of the Immigration and Nationality Act, which upholds the quota system set in 1921–24 but removes race as a bar to immigration and naturalization and removes discrimination between sexes. The act gives preference to immigrants with special skills needed in the United States, provides for more rigorous screening of immigrants in order to eliminate people considered to be subversive (particularly communists and homosexuals), and allows broader grounds for the deportation of criminal aliens.

1953 The television program *Make Room for Daddy*, starring comic actor **Danny Thomas**, debuts on the ABC network.

1954 As jobs in the United States become harder to find, Mexican workers are viewed as unwanted competition by many. Under Operation Wetback, a special government force locates undocumented workers and forces them to return to Mexico. In one year alone, about one million people of Mexican descent are deported.

1959 The Cuban Revolution initiates a mass migration from Cuba to the United States—more than one million Cubans will immigrate after this year.

1960 Romanian and Jewish immigrant **Elie Wiesel**'s memoir *Night* is published. The book, which describes Wiesel's experiences in the Nazi concentration camps, will sell more than five million copies throughout the world and will be translated into thirty languages.

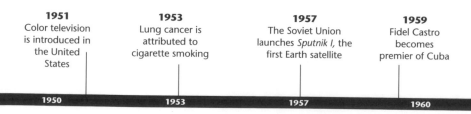

1951
Color television is introduced in the United States

1953
Lung cancer is attributed to cigarette smoking

1957
The Soviet Union launches *Sputnik I*, the first Earth satellite

1959
Fidel Castro becomes premier of Cuba

1950   1953   1957   1960

1960–80 The Filipino population in the United States more than quadruples, from 176,130 to 781,894.

1960s Between 4 and 5 million African Americans have migrated from the South to the North since the turn of the century.

1962 Hawaiian voters elect World War II hero **Daniel K. Inouye** as their senator. He becomes the first American of Japanese descent to serve in the U.S. Congress.

1962 Comic actor Danny Thomas dedicates the St. Jude's Children's Research Hospital, in Memphis, Tennessee.

1963 Civil rights activist **Yuri Kochiyama** meets Malcolm X and joins his group, the Organization for Afro-American Unity.

1963 **Daniel Patrick Moynihan** and fellow professor Nathan Glazer write *Beyond the Melting Pot,* a book challenging the belief that immigrants to the United States mix with other cultures and form an "American" identity.

1965 In a new spirit of immigration reform, Congress repeals the national-origins quotas and gives each Eastern Hemisphere nation an annual quota of 20,000, excluding immediate family members of U.S. citizens. The Eastern Hemisphere receives 170,000 places for immigrants and the Western Hemisphere 120,000. (In 1978, Congress creates a worldwide immigration system by combining the two hemispheres.)

1966–80 About 14,000 Dominicans per year enter the United States, most seeking employment they cannot find at home.

1968 Japanese native **Yoko Ono** meets Beatle John Lennon at an exhibit of her artwork; they marry within a year.

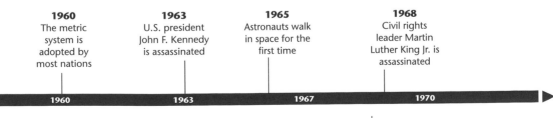

1960
The metric system is adopted by most nations

1963
U.S. president John F. Kennedy is assassinated

1965
Astronauts walk in space for the first time

1968
Civil rights leader Martin Luther King Jr. is assassinated

1960   1963   1967   1970

1970 The campaign against grape growers, led by union leader **César Chávez**, finally succeeds; after a successful grape boycott, a group of California growers signs an agreement with the United Farm Workers, giving grape pickers higher wages.

1972–81 Sailboats carrying Haitians begin to arrive on the shores of Florida. More than 55,000 Haitian "boat people"—and perhaps more than 100,000—arrive in this wave.

1973 Henry Kissinger, U.S. secretary of state and a major influence in U.S. foreign policy, wins the Nobel Peace Prize.

1975 Saigon, the South Vietnamese capital, falls to the communist North on April 30; at least 65,000 South Vietnamese immediately flee the country.

1975–81 About 123,600 Laotian refugees enter the United States.

1976 Daniel Patrick Moynihan is elected as a U.S. senator from New York and serves for twenty-four years.

1977 Palestine native **Edward Said** is elected to the Palestine National Council (PNC) and begins his work to seek a peaceful agreement between Palestinians and Israelis.

1977 **Josie Natori** leaves a successful career in finance to design a line of sleepwear using materials and design work from her native Philippines. She generates $150,000 worth of orders in only a few months.

1979 In the aftermath of the Vietnam War, the Orderly Departure Program (ODP) is established to provide a safe alternative for Vietnamese people who are fleeing the country in large numbers, often risking their lives in

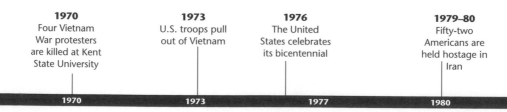

1970
Four Vietnam War protesters are killed at Kent State University

1973
U.S. troops pull out of Vietnam

1976
The United States celebrates its bicentennial

1979–80
Fifty-two Americans are held hostage in Iran

1970   1973   1977   1980

overcrowded old boats. Under the ODP, refugees are allowed to leave Vietnam directly for resettlement in one of two dozen countries, including the United States. There are about 165,000 admissions to the United States under the ODP by 1989, and new arrivals continue into the 1990s.

1980 More than 125,000 Cubans flee to the United States during the Mariel Boat Lift.

1980–86 Tens of thousands of Cambodian refugees enter the United States annually.

1981–2000 The United States accepts 531,310 Vietnamese refugees.

1982 Peru native **Isabel Allende** wins international acclaim for *La casa de los espíritus*. Three years later, the novel is published in English as *The House of the Spirits*.

1982 In *Plyler v. Doe,* the U.S. Supreme Court rules that the children of illegal immigrants have the same rights as everyone else, especially the right to an education.

1983 Chinese-born architect **I. M. Pei** receives the prestigious Prizker Architecture Prize and uses the $100,000 award to establish a scholarship fund for Chinese students to study architecture in the United States.

1984 Austrian immigrant **Arnold Schwarzenegger** stars in the successful futuristic film *The Terminator*.

1984 New York governor **Mario Cuomo** delivers a memorable keynote address at the Democratic National Convention. The speech includes the story of his immigrant family's efforts to make a good life in America and raises awareness of the need for political programs to help the less fortunate.

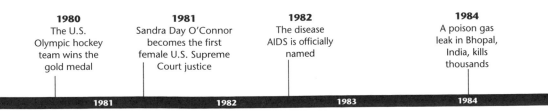

1980
The U.S. Olympic hockey team wins the gold medal

1981
Sandra Day O'Connor becomes the first female U.S. Supreme Court justice

1982
The disease AIDS is officially named

1984
A poison gas leak in Bhopal, India, kills thousands

1981　1982　1983　1984

1985 Mexican native **Antonia Hernández** becomes president of the Mexican American Legal Defense and Educational Fund (MALDEF), vowing to ensure equal opportunity to all Latinos. She works to support bilingual education and challenge anti-immigrant laws.

1986 The Immigration Reform and Control Act (IRCA) provides amnesty (pardon to a group of people) to more than 3 million undocumented immigrants who had entered the United States before 1982, allowing them to become legal residents. The measure outlaws the knowing employment of undocumented immigrants and makes it more difficult for undocumented immigrants to receive public assistance.

1988 Congress passes the Amerasian Homecoming Act, which brings thousands of children—most are the offspring of American servicemen and Asian mothers—to the United States.

1989 **Le Ly Hayslip** becomes nationally famous in the United States when her first book, *When Heaven and Earth Changed Places,* is published. The book chronicles her experiences as a girl growing up during the Vietnam War.

1991–93 Some 43,000 Haitians try to reach the United States by boat. Many of their boats are intercepted by U.S. officials and those emigrants are taken to Guantánamo Bay, a U.S. naval base in Cuba.

1993 **John Shalikashvili**, a Polish-born member of the U.S. Army, is chosen to become chairman of the Joint Chiefs by President Bill Clinton.

1994 In an effort to stop undocumented workers from illegally crossing the border, the government adopts Operation Gatekeeper, an extensive border patrol system

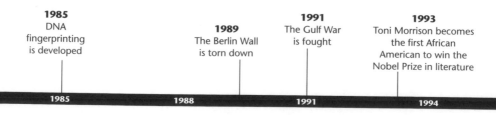

1985
DNA fingerprinting is developed

1989
The Berlin Wall is torn down

1991
The Gulf War is fought

1993
Toni Morrison becomes the first African American to win the Nobel Prize in literature

1985   1988   1991   1994

at Imperial Beach at the border between Mexico and southern California. The number of border agents is increased and new hi-tech equipment is put to use, costing billions of dollars over the next few years. Illegal immigration moves further inland where the climate is more severe, proving to be deadly in some cases.

1994   The United States enters a Wet Feet–Dry Feet agreement with Cuba under which, if fleeing Cubans trying to reach the United States are caught at sea, U.S. authorities will send them back to Cuba. If the Cubans make it to U.S. shores, they will be admitted to the country.

1994   California citizens vote in favor of Proposition 187, a law designed to stop immigrants without visas from receiving public benefits from the state; a judge later blocks the state from putting the proposition into effect.

1996   Congress passes the Illegal Immigration Reform and Immigrant Responsibility Act (IIRIRA). The IIRIRA creates a huge increase in funding for border patrol personnel and equipment. This act creates harsher penalties for illegal immigration, restricts welfare benefits to recent immigrants, and makes the deportation process easier for U.S. administrators. The IIRIRA also tries to make it harder for foreign terrorists to enter the United States.

1996   The bombing of the Oklahoma Federal Building at the hands of a terrorist (a U.S. citizen) in 1995 raises new fears about terrorism. The Anti-terrorism Act is passed, making deportation automatic if an immigrant commits a deportable felony (a grave crime), even if the immigrant has been in the United States

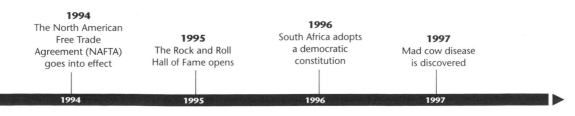

1994
The North American Free Trade Agreement (NAFTA) goes into effect

1995
The Rock and Roll Hall of Fame opens

1996
South Africa adopts a democratic constitution

1997
Mad cow disease is discovered

| 1994 | 1995 | 1996 | 1997 |

since early childhood. By 2003, 500,000 people had been deported under the terms of this act.

1997 Czech native **Madeleine Albright** assumes the role of U.S. secretary of state during the administration of Bill Clinton. She becomes the highest-ranking woman in the U.S. government at that time, and the first woman in U.S. history to hold that title.

1997 The Border Patrol initiates Operation Rio Grande, strengthening the Texas-Mexico border with more agents to deter people from crossing.

1998 California passes Proposition 227, a referendum that bans bilingual classroom education and English as a second language (ESL) program, replacing them with a one-year intensive English immersion program.

2000 The Immigration and Naturalization Service estimates the number of undocumented immigrants in the country at about 7 million, up from the estimate of 5.8 million in 1996. About 70 percent of the undocumented immigrants are from Mexico.

2001 Congress passes the USA PATRIOT Act ("Uniting and Strengthening America by Providing Appropriate Tools Required to Intercept and Obstruct Terrorism"). The bill calls for increased border patrol and tightened provisions for screening and restricting immigrants. It grants sweeping new powers to federal police agencies and permits indefinite detention of immigrants and aliens in the country for minor immigration status violations.

2001 Within weeks of the September 11 terrorist attacks on New York and Washington, D.C., approximately 1,200 immigrants are arrested by federal government agents as part of an anti-terrorist campaign. Most are from Saudi

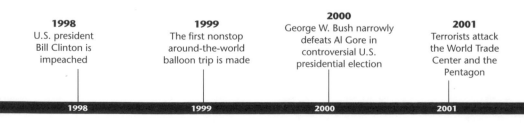

1998
U.S. president Bill Clinton is impeached

1999
The first nonstop around-the-world balloon trip is made

2000
George W. Bush narrowly defeats Al Gore in controversial U.S. presidential election

2001
Terrorists attack the World Trade Center and the Pentagon

1998   1999   2000   2001

Arabia, Egypt, and Pakistan. Many are held without charges and without access to attorneys or their families. Many are deported. None are charged with terrorism.

2002 The Homeland Security Department requires the annual registration of temporary male immigrants from twenty-four predominantly Arab or Muslim countries as well as North Korea. People from the following countries are required to register: Afghanistan, Algeria, Bahrain, Eritrea, Iran, Iraq, Lebanon, Libya, Morocco, North Korea, Oman, Pakistan, Qatar, Saudi Arabia, Somalia, Sudan, Syria, Tunisia, United Arab Emirates, and Yemen. The following year, five more countries are added to the list: Bangladesh, Egypt, Indonesia, Jordan, and Kuwait. Of the 83,519 people who register with immigration officials in 2002, 13,799 are put in deportation proceedings. Others complain of terrifying or humiliating interrogations and harsh conditions. Immigrant and civil liberties groups protest the policy.

2002 Conservative talk-show host and former presidential candidate **Patrick J. Buchanan** publishes *The Death of the West: How Dying Populations and Immigrant Invasions Imperil Our Country and Civilization,* in which he warns that immigration and low birth rates would result in white people being a minority in the United States, where they once constituted an overwhelming majority.

2003 The explosion of space shuttle *Columbia* takes the life of **Kalpana Chawla**, the first female astronaut from India, and the lives of her six fellow crew members.

2003 Actor Arnold Schwarzenegger is elected governor of California.

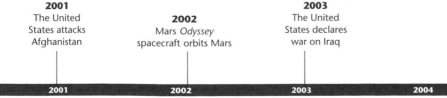

2001
The United
States attacks
Afghanistan

2002
Mars *Odyssey*
spacecraft orbits Mars

2003
The United
States declares
war on Iraq

2001   2002   2003   2004

U.S. Immigration and Migration
Biographies

Henry Kissinger

Born May 27, 1923
Füurth, Germany

U.S. secretary of state and
foreign policy expert

Henry Kissinger, who immigrated to the United States as a teenager, was one of the most powerful American officials during the presidencies of Richard M. Nixon (1913–1994; served 1969–74) and Gerald R. Ford (1913–; served 1974–77). He is widely credited with negotiating an end to the Vietnam War (1954–75), as well as opening a new era of improved relations with the Soviet Union (a country made up of fifteen republics, the largest of which was Russia, that in 1991 became independent states) and the People's Republic of China. Critics of Kissinger, however, also blamed him for supporting the brutal anticommunist policies of governments in South America that resulted in violations of human rights. Kissinger, who came to the United States as a child refugee from Nazi Germany in 1938, won the Nobel Peace Prize in 1973 for his work in ending the Vietnam War.

"There cannot be a crisis next week. My schedule is already full."

Henry Kissinger. *AP/Wide World Photos.*

Beginnings in Germany

Alfred Heinz (Henry) Kissinger was born in Füurth, Germany, in 1923, the son of a Jewish schoolteacher. In 1933, the Nazi Party led by Adolf Hitler (1889–1945) came to power in Germany, partly on the strength of the party's strong anti-Jewish program. Soon, Jews were prohibited from certain professions, including teaching, and the Kissinger family fled Germany for the United States in 1938, just ahead of the brutal Holocaust that ended with the killing of millions of Jews in Europe. Kissinger was fifteen when he and his family left their native country.

The Kissinger family resettled in New York City, where young Henry went to high school, attending classes at night while working in a shaving-brush factory during the day. In 1941, Kissinger enrolled in the City College of New York as an accounting student while still working full time. He was drafted into the U.S. Army during World War II (1939–45), and he was assigned to deliver lectures to American troops on the objectives of the United States in the war. As a result of his talks, Kissinger was recruited to become a member of the Army's intelligence division. He later worked with American troops occupying Germany after the defeat of the Nazi government.

After the war, in 1947, Kissinger enrolled in Harvard University, where he graduated in 1950. He later earned advanced degrees, including a doctorate in philosophy (in 1954) at Harvard, and joined the university's faculty. In the 1960s, Kissinger began consulting with New York governor Nelson A. Rockefeller (1908–1979), who was seeking the Republican presidential nomination in 1968. Rockefeller lost out to Richard Nixon, who then defeated Vice President Hubert Humphrey (1911–1978) in the general election. Nixon asked Kissinger to become his national security advisor. (A national security advisor is an expert in foreign affairs who works in the White House rather than at the State Department.) Under Nixon, Kissinger became more influential than the secretary of state in formulating American policy at a time when competition with the Soviet Union was at the heart of U.S. policy.

It was also a time when the United States seemed to be in a stalemate with communist rebels in Vietnam, and Nixon had promised in his successful 1968 election campaign to end the war. Negotiating an end to the conflict fell to Kissinger.

Nobel Peace Prize

The Vietnam War became a turning point in American history. Starting gradually with a few troops in the early 1960s, the involvement by the United States in trying to prevent domination of South Vietnam by communist troops from the North had become a full-scale war by the late 1960s. The war was highly unpopular with the American public, and Nixon had been elected president in 1968 on a promise to negotiate an end to the fighting. In fact, it took Kissinger more than four years to conclude a peace treaty with North Vietnam, and not long afterwards, communist forces took control over the entire country. By any measure, American policy had failed.

Nevertheless, Kissinger shared the prestigious Nobel Peace Prize with his North Vietnamese counterpart, Le Duc Tho (1911–1990), in 1973. In his acceptance speech for the prize, Kissinger declared: "To the realist, peace represents a stable arrangement of power." The United States had in fact

U.S. secretary of state Henry Kissinger (left) meets with North Vietnam foreign minister Le Duc Tho (far right) at the Paris Peace Talks in 1973. *National Archives and Records Administration.*

Henry Kissinger and the Nobel Peace Prize

The Nobel Foundation of Oslo, Norway, annually awards the Nobel Peace Prize to diplomats or world leaders who, in its opinion, have contributed to the cause of world peace. Ironically, the prize is funded from the fortune of Alfred Nobel (1833–1896), who invented dynamite. In 1973, the peace prize was shared by Henry Kissinger of the United States and Le Duc Tho, the foreign minister of North Vietnam, for their role in negotiating an end to the fighting in the long Vietnam War.

The Nobel Committee, in presenting the prize, observed that "we are under no illusion that the differences between systems and ideologies can be ignored [that is, between the communist North Vietnam and the capitalist United States]; but the Nobel Committee has been anxious to emphasize that in a world yearning for peace, no one can assume the right to force his particular system on others by armed might. Nations with different systems of government must be able to live together in peace and solve their controversies [differences] by negotiation."

In his acceptance speech, Kissinger seemed to reflect the same idea: "To the realist, peace represents a stable arrangement of power."

Kissinger's remark struck some people as a distinct departure for American foreign policy, which seemed to have been based on a belief of what was thought to be "right": the idea of democratically elected governments, guarantees of free speech, and freedom to own property. Kissinger seemed to be saying that in diplomacy, what mattered was "power," which might be based on the force of arms (such as by the police) rather than on the will of the people. It was, to many, a viewpoint that seemed more at home in Europe than in the United States. It was also a viewpoint that helped turn the United States toward a policy of negotiating peaceful arrangements with governments that held power, rather than refusing to deal with such governments (as in the case of China) because of their political beliefs or the manner in which they achieved power (through violence, for example, rather than through elections).

lost the war in Vietnam, and the loss pointed Kissinger in a new direction in American foreign policy, particularly in relations with the Soviet Union and China, which was ruled by the Chinese Communist Party.

Prior to Vietnam, American foreign policy had been dedicated to the notion of combating communism wherever the political philosophy gained power. The United States and the Soviet Union, the world's most powerful communist government, had been engaged in a back-and-forth struggle for world power and influence since 1945, the end of World War II. American policy towards China had been hostile since the victory of communist fighters in China in 1948; in fact, the United States officially maintained that the legitimate government of mainland China was situated on the Pacific island of Taiwan, a province of China where anticommunist Chinese had fled.

Kissinger introduced a new concept to American foreign policy: dealing with governments as they existed, while effectively dropping a long-standing crusade against communism. Consequently, it was partly as a result of Kissinger's urging that President Nixon, who had made his early political reputation as a strong anticommunist in the late 1940s and 1950s, made a surprise diplomatic visit to China in 1972, and a separate trip to the Soviet Union later the same year. Nixon's visit to China led directly to the opening of formal diplomatic relations between the two countries, and his visit to the Soviet Union led to a treaty under which the two countries agreed to control their buildup of nuclear weapons.

Nixon sank into political problems as a result of a scandal called Watergate, in which agents of Nixon's reelection campaign had broken into the headquarters of the opposition Democratic Party in June 1972. Kissinger emerged as a stable leader of the government in foreign policy. After Nixon resigned office in the face of almost certain impeachment (the formal accusation of a public official charged with misconduct and the trial that follows), Kissinger continued in his role of secretary of state under Nixon's successor, Gerald Ford.

Kissinger the man

Kissinger brought a distinctive personality to his job. He had never lost a distinctive German accent while speaking English, and his slow, careful delivery of heavily accented English was unique. Presiding over American foreign policy at a time of domestic political chaos made Kissinger seem like a figure of stability in government.

His style did not prevent him from becoming a highly controversial figure, however. Although Kissinger's world policy was based on the notion that the Soviet Union should be allowed to dominate other communist countries, in cases where communists tried to gain influence elsewhere, such as in Chile, Kissinger was swift to take action to maintain what he regarded as the American sphere of influence. When communists appeared to be gaining too much influence over Chile's government for Kissinger's taste, the United States secretly supported the military takeover of the government in Santiago in 1973. The president of Chile, Salvador Allende (1908–1973), who had been elected democratically, was killed. Kissinger was roundly criticized for supporting an antidemocratic *coup d'état,* or the violent overthrow of a government by a small group, in the South American country.

Out of office

In 1976, Democrat Jimmy Carter (1924–; served 1977–81) of Georgia defeated Gerald Ford in the presidential election, and Kissinger left office. Although he was consulted after later Republicans Ronald Reagan (1911–; served 1981–89) and George Bush (1924–; served 1989–93) were elected in three consecutive elections (1980, 1984, and 1988), Kissinger did not return to office. Instead, he established a consulting firm for large American corporations doing business overseas.

Kissinger enjoyed enormous prestige while in office. In later years, however, Kissinger's reputation was mixed. On the one hand, he negotiated a peace agreement with North Vietnam; on the other hand, communist Vietnamese soon afterwards seized control of the entire country, making the Vietnam War, and the fifty-five thousand American deaths in the war, seem pointless. The American role in aiding the bloody military takeover of Chile's government, which had been democratically elected, seemed to contradict the country's long vision of itself as the defender of democracy over military dictatorships.

Kissinger was also widely credited for maintaining the stability of American foreign policy during the period when his boss, President Nixon, was under increasing political attack for the Watergate affair. Kissinger's defenders credit him with persuading Nixon to adopt a more realistic attitude towards the world's most populous nation, China, and towards the other nuclear-armed superpower, the Soviet Union, thereby helping promote more stable international relations.

—*James L. Outman*

For More Information

Books

Isaacson, Walter. *Kissinger: A Biography.* New York: Simon & Schuster, 1992.

Israel, Fred L. *Henry Kissinger.* New York: Chelsea House, 1986.

Kissinger, Henry. *Years of Renewal.* New York: Simon & Schuster, 1999.

Kissinger, Henry. *Years of Upheaval.* Boston: Little, Brown, 1982.

Schulzinger, Robert D. *Henry Kissinger: Doctor of Diplomacy.* New York: Columbia University Press, 1988.

Periodicals

"Getting Out Is Never Easy." *The Economist* (March 1, 2003).

Hersh, Seymour. "The Price of Power, Kissinger, Nixon and Chile." *The Atlantic* (December 1982): p. 31.

Hitchens, Christopher. "The Case Against Henry Kissinger." *Harper's Magazine* (March 2001): p. 49.

Lacqueur, Walter. "Kissinger and His Critics." *Commentary* (February 1980): p. 57.

Web Sites

Chaundy, Bob. "Henry Kissinger: Haunted By His Past." *BBC News.* http://news.bbc.co.uk/2/hi/in_depth/uk/2000/newsmakers/1952981.stm (accessed on March 18, 2004).

"Henry Kissinger—Biography." *Nobel e-Museum.* http://www.nobel.se/peace/laureates/1973/kissinger-bio.html (accessed on March 18, 2004).

PBS. "The Trials of Henry Kissinger." *Now with Bill Moyers.* http://www.pbs.org/now/politics/kissinger.html (accessed on March 18, 2004).

Yuri Kochiyama

Born May 19, 1922
San Pedro, California

Activist and speaker

"Don't become too narrow. Live fully. Meet all kinds of people. You'll learn something from everyone. Follow what you feel in your heart."

Yuri Kochiyama. *Yuri Kochiyama.*

As a teenager, Yuri Kochiyama lived a quiet life in small-town San Pedro, California. She wanted to be a teacher and had no interest in political issues or life much beyond her local, middle-class community. That all changed after the surprise attack in December 1941 on Pearl Harbor, Hawaii, by Japanese forces. Within weeks, the U.S. government forced over 120,000 people of Japanese ancestry—70 percent of whom were American-born citizens—to leave their homes and move to internment camps, where people were held in custody during a war. That experience was the inspiration for Kochiyama's political activism for social justice, civil rights, and racial equality.

Kochiyama's activism took root during the 1960s, when she became involved in many causes and groups, including membership in the Organization for Afro-American Unity (OAAU). She became a close friend of Malcolm X (1925–1965), whose aggressive approach to racism contrasted with the civil disobedience (disobeying unjust laws in a peaceful manner) of Dr. Martin Luther King Jr. (1929–1968). In a famous photograph, Kochiyama is shown holding Malcolm X, the Nation of Islam leader, after he was shot and killed in 1965.

Rounded up

Yuri Kochiyama was born Mary Nakahara in 1922 in San Pedro, California, a port town just south of Los Angeles. Her father, Seiichi Nakahara, had immigrated to America by himself. On a return visit to Japan, he met a teacher at the school where his father was principal. They married and settled in San Pedro, where Nakahara owned a fish market. Kochiyama had a twin brother and an older brother.

Kochiyama was quiet and obedient as a youth. While in high school, she taught Sunday school classes and performed volunteer work with the Young Women's Christian Association (YMCA) and the Girl Scouts of America. She was attending a junior (two-year) college when the Japanese military bombed the American naval station at Pearl Harbor, Hawaii. That day, agents from the Federal Bureau of Investigation (FBI) came to her family's home. She was at home caring for her father, who was in bed recuperating after having had surgery on his stomach the day before. The agents arrested her father, and he was taken to a nearby federal prison. When his health began worsening, her father was moved to a hospital, and then he was returned home on January 20, 1942. He died the next day. The family received a warning from FBI agents that if they had a funeral for their father the event would be under surveillance, or observation. At the time, travel by Japanese people was limited to five miles. Despite the restrictions, many family friends attended the funeral.

Soon afterwards, Kochiyama and her mother were among the Japanese Americans shipped by cars, trains, and buses to internment camps. The Kochiyamas were sent to an internment camp in Jerome, Arkansas. Mother and daughter lived in barracks, or buildings designed to hold groups of soldiers, with other families. Each person in the camp had a job in order to enable the camp to run by itself. The experience forged Kochiyama's commitment to overcome the race-based assumptions that had led the U.S. government to round up Japanese Americans.

In being forced away from the small community where she grew up, Kochiyama saw that similar racial assumptions were being applied in different ways to other minority groups. As she traveled to the camp, for example, she noticed racial segregation in Southern states—from diners with signs announcing they did not serve people of color to differences in the living conditions of white and black communities.

While Kochiyama was in Arkansas, the camp was visited by the Japanese American 442nd regimental combat team. Young Americans of Japanese ancestry had petitioned U.S. president Franklin D. Roosevelt (1882–1945; served 1933–45) to be permitted to serve their country in World War II (1939–45). After several months of consideration, Roosevelt issued an executive order establishing a special army combat team consisting of Japanese American volunteers, the 442nd regimental combat team. Future U.S. senator Daniel K. Inouye (1924–; see entry in volume 1) of Hawaii was on that team.

In preparation for their visit to the camp, Kochiyama worked as a receptionist. She sat at a desk, registered each soldier, and was responsible for assigning them with lodging. Since almost all the men were from Hawaii, she asked each man for his name, rank—and home island. One soldier replied, "Manhattan Island," since he was from New York City. When Kochiyama asked about his family, the soldier replied that he had sixty brothers and sixty sisters, then explained that he grew up in an orphanage.

When the regiment left for Europe, Kochiyama promised that soldier she would write to him every day. The soldier, Bill Kochiyama, would later become her husband. Soon, Bill wrote back to Kochiyama that he was embarrassed to receive so many letters when some of his fellow soldiers received none. He asked Kochiyama to write to other men as well. She organized fellow inmates to write letters so that none of the soldiers in the squad would go without mail.

Kochiyama comes to Harlem

After the war was over, the couple reunited in New York. On their first date, Kochiyama invited Bill to come to the Sunday school where she was teaching. She made Bill teach the kids a popular new dance he learned in Europe—the "lindy hop." After one more date, the couple was married. They would have six children.

From 1948 to 1960, the Kochiyamas lived in a New York housing project. They moved to a newly built housing project in Harlem in 1960. Harlem had become an impoverished community. Kochiyama's attempts to improve some basic safety needs and city services led Kochiyama to first became a social activist—near the time of her fortieth birthday. She worked with other parents for safer streets, including reduced speed limits, and for integrated education. In addition, she became politically active, first by attending meetings of people who had recently returned from Cuba. The Cuban Revolution of the 1950s resulted in a break in Cuban-American relations and Cuba becoming a communist country. (Communism is a political philosophy that advocates government ownership and control of businesses and farms, and a nearly equal distribution of income.)

Meanwhile, the civil rights movement was gaining momentum in the United States during this period. Many of Kochiyama's friends participated in Freedom Rides: People from different parts of the country would travel for civil rights marches in communities in the South that still practiced segregation, the separation of races. Two of her children participated in the Freedom Rides, one of them through the Student Non-Violent Coordinating Committee, and the other through a group called Students Against Social Injustice. Kochiyama herself was involved in various protest demonstrations.

In 1963, she met civil rights advocate Malcolm X and joined his group, the Organization for Afro-American Unity, to work for racial justice and human rights. Through Kochiyama, Malcolm X, in turn, met with members of the Hiroshima-Nagasaki World Peace Study Mission. The group, which spoke out against the proliferation of nuclear weapons, was named after the two Japanese cities that had been hit with atomic bombs near the end of World War II. They met during an event in Harlem called the "World's Worst Fair." The Harlem fair was meant to contrast with the World's Fair being held at that time in Flushing Meadows, New York. On display at the World's Fair were examples of modern progress from all over the world. The World's Worst Fair, on the other hand, showed poor living conditions in the richest country on Earth. Pointing to decaying and burned-out buildings in Harlem, Malcolm X said to the members of the Hiroshima-Nagasaki World Peace Study Mission, "You have been bombed and you saw that we have been bombed, too ... by racism."

Friendship and respect were mutual between Kochiyama and Malcolm X. In 1965, they would be linked one final time—in a photograph published in magazines and newspapers around the world in which Kochiyama was seen holding Malcolm X after he was shot by a fellow member of the Nation of Islam at the Audubon Ballroom in Harlem.

Social activism became even more heated in Harlem during the mid-1960s, with protests against the Vietnam War (1954–75) and racism, and for civil rights and women's rights. The murder of Malcolm X in 1965 intensified Kochiyama's commitment to work for dignity and equality for all people. She supported the work of the Black Panther Party, which pursued separation of African Americans from mainstream American society.

A life of activism

Kochiyama became a leading speaker and organizer of demonstrations for various causes, including protests against the Vietnam War and marches for women's rights, and from gatherings intended to draw attention to neighborhood problems to demonstrations over international issues. She took part in the takeover of the Statue of Liberty in 1977, for example, to demand freedom for Puerto Ricans imprisoned for their political beliefs. Among her most personal causes, she rallied for reparations for people of Japanese descent who were held captive during World War II and lost their businesses, savings, and jobs. Her husband, Bill Kochiyama, testified at a government commission in Washington, D.C., that was formed to investigate the internment camps. In 1988, President Ronald Reagan (1911–; served 1981–89) signed an act that provided an apology and $20,000 to each surviving internee. By then, almost half of the internees had died. The Kochiyamas continued to protest when the act did not address a related group of people who had been confined in internment camps, Latin Americans of Japanese ancestry.

Elderly and active

When her husband died in 1993, Kochiyama lost her strongest and longest supporter, a man who took pride in his wife when she was arrested in demonstrations for social justice. In 1997, she suffered a stroke, which weakened her legs significantly. She left Harlem in 1999, after thirty years of local and national activism, and returned to her native state of California, where most of her children had settled. Kochiyama moved to the Bay Area and quickly became a high-profile activist for local causes in Oakland and San Francisco as well as for national and international rights issues.

Among international causes, she attended and spoke at rallies on behalf of Peru and the Philippines, where she believed European and American influence continued to dominate those countries. She spoke out against detainment, or holding without charging with a crime, of hundreds of Middle Easterners following the terrorist attacks of September 11, 2001. "She wants to be certain that Muslims and Arab Americans will not struggle alone, as she and other Japanese Americans once did," noted Ryan Kim in an article in the *San Francisco Chronicle*. "We [Japanese Americans] went through some similar things in World War II when we were evacuated and incarcerated," Kochiyama said to Kim.

Kochiyama continued to participate as an activist after turning eighty in 2002, alternating between visits for physical therapy with meetings of such groups as People's Resistance Against U.S. Terrorism. Still a featured speaker at rallies and participant in marches, even though she had to use a walker, Kochiyama continued to address injustices she perceived. Explaining why demonstrations are important, she stated, "If they did not have all those years of marching and demonstrations, they never would have gotten the Civil Rights Act of 1964.... I like it because it's a people's thing. It's not an individual thing. It's all the things that people do together that gives you strength."

—*Roger Matuz*

For More Information

Books
Kochiyama, Yuri (author of preface). *Dragon Ladies: Asian American Feminists Breathe Fire*. Edited by Sonia Shah. Boston: South End, 1997.

Periodicals
Kim, Ryan. "Japanese Americans Fight Backlash; Peace Rally Opposes Ethnic Scapegoats." *San Francisco Chronicle* (October 2, 2001): p. A2.

Videotapes

Yuri Kochiyama: Passion for Justice. Video National Asian American Telecommunications Association, 1993.

Web Sites

Hung, Melissa. "Yuri Kochiyama: The Last Revolutionary." *Model Minority.* http://modelminority.com/article364.html (accessed on March 18, 2004).

"Yuri Kochiyama." *National Women's History Project.* http://www.nwhp.org/tlp/biographies/kochiyama/kochiyama-bio.html (accessed on March 18, 2004).

"Yuri Kochiyama: With Justice in Her Heart." *Revolutionary Worker Online.* http://rwor.org/a/v20/980-89/986/yuri.htm (accessed on March 18, 2004).

Emma Lazarus

Born July 22, 1849
New York, New York

Died November 19, 1887
New York, New York

**Author of the famous poem that appears
on the pedestal of the Statue of Liberty,
and Jewish rights advocate**

If Emma Lazarus had done nothing else in life, writing the poem "The New Colossus" would have preserved her name in American history. Engraved on the pedestal of the **Statue of Liberty** (see entry in volume 2) in New York Harbor, the poem seems to capture the spirit of the woman holding a torch aloft, as if to light the way for the flood of European immigrants streaming into the United States when the lines were written in 1883: "Give me your tired, your poor, / Your huddled masses yearning to breathe free, / The wretched refuse of your teeming shore. / Send these, the homeless, tempest-tost to me. / I lift my lamp beside the golden door." The facts that lie behind the poem, and its author, reveal the much greater complexities of immigration to the United States.

"Give me your tired, your poor, Your huddled masses yearning to breathe free…"

Growing up in New York

Emma Lazarus grew up in a privileged household in New York City. Her family was descended from Sephardic Jews, a large community that lived in Spain and Portugal during the Middle Ages (about 500–1400). In 1492, the same year

Emma Lazarus.
© *Bettmann/Corbis.*

that Christopher Columbus (1451–1506) discovered the Western Hemisphere on a voyage paid for by the king and queen of Spain, the Jews were expelled from Spain, part of a program by the Catholic Church to ensure that everyone accepted the same religion. At first, some Jews went to neighboring Portugal, but they were also expelled from that country. Eventually, some Sephardic Jews traveled to the Portuguese colony of Brazil, and from there some made their way to New York years before the American Revolution of 1776.

In Spain, the Sephardic Jews had been integrated into the larger society, unlike Jews in northern Europe, notably Germany, who had been forced to live apart from the Christian population. One result was that Sephardic Jews expected to participate in the society around them, and Emma Lazarus's family was no exception. Her father, Moses Lazarus, was a wealthy businessman who had friends in the upper class of New York City society. He belonged to exclusive social clubs, such as the Union Club, and built an elaborate summer house in Newport, Rhode Island, where other socially prominent New York families also owned homes.

Emma Lazarus did not attend school; her education was provided by private tutors hired by her father. She grew up in a family that valued culture—painting, music, and literature—and she took pride in her heritage, which reached back to a time when Spain was a scientific and cultural leader. But as she was growing up, winds of change were blowing across the Atlantic and through the streets of New York.

The surge in immigration

Starting just a few years before Lazarus was born, a new surge of immigrants had started coming to the United States, and to New York in particular. These were Germans who had been hurt by both widespread crop failures and by political unrest that resulted from the rapid growth of industry in Germany. From Ireland came another enormous wave of immigrants, driven from their land by the failure of the potato crop, the main source of food. Unlike most earlier immigrants to the United States, Protestants who had come from England and Scotland, many of the new immigrants in the 1840s and 1850s were Catholics. Most were poor. In the case of the Irish, some families had spent their last money on buying tickets to sail to New York in order to escape death by starvation. This new wave of poor, Catholic immigrants disturbed some Americans, who feared that the Catholic Church would try to exert influence over American politics by directing the votes of Irish immigrants who became citizens. Anti-Catholic riots occurred in several East Coast cities, and Catholic churches were attacked and burned.

A movement of native-born Americans who called themselves Know Nothings (because, when asked about their movement, they replied: "I know nothing") began campaigning for restrictions on immigration, a much longer waiting period to become a citizen, and a ban on foreign-born people holding public office. In California, where large numbers of Chinese had arrived looking for gold during the California Gold Rush of 1848, similar anti-immigrant sentiments arose, directed against the Chinese.

In most respects, Lazarus was little affected by the rising tide of religious intolerance. Most of her friends were Christians, and her immediate family was even shunned by other members of the Sephardic Jewish community for their failure to observe the practices and customs of Judaism (the religion of Jews, who believe in the Old Testament of the Bible). In the meantime, Lazarus was building a reputation as a writer and a poet. When she was sixteen, her father paid to publish a collection of her poems, *Poems and Translations Written Between the Ages of Fourteen and Seventeen.* Critics kindly described the poems of the sort often written by young women of Lazarus's age. Nevertheless, the self-confident Lazarus sent a copy to Ralph Waldo Emerson (1803–1882) in Concord, Massachusetts, who was one of the most prominent American poets then living. He replied, and Lazarus and Emerson maintained a long correspondence, marked by at least two invitations by Emerson for Lazarus to visit him at his home.

Lazarus published a second book of poems, *Admetus and Other Poems,* in 1871, and it received more positive reviews. The *Illustrated London News* said she was "a poet of rare original power." Lazarus continued publishing books, including a novel, *Alide: An Episode in Goethe's Life,* published in 1874, as well as a steady stream of poems published in popular magazines. In 1876, Lazarus completed a play, *The Spagnoletto,* which was privately published but never performed. In addition to her collections of poems, Lazarus also published magazine articles about the arts and literature. She occasionally toured Europe. Her name was well known and respected among the important writers of the era.

Despite her success and acceptance, she was aware of a social undercurrent of anti-Semitism, or anti-Jew, an attitude that came to the surface in the summer of 1877. In Saratoga, New York, a fashionable summer resort for New Yorkers, the owner of the Grand Union Hotel refused to accept as a guest Joseph Seligman (1819–1880), a well-known Jewish banker from New York. The hotel owner, Judge Henry Hilton (1824–1899), explained that he thought Christians did not want to stay in the same hotel as Jews, and that this was hurting his business. It was an era before laws prohibited discrimination, and although the hotel owner insisted that his policy was really aimed at Jews from Germany, rather than the long-established Sephardic Jews, the incident marked a turning point in the life of Lazarus. Although her family had not been turned away, the hotel's policy showed that Jews were not regarded in the same light as others in society. Lazarus later wrote to a friend that she was "perfectly conscious that this contempt and hatred underlies the general tone of the community towards us [Jews]."

Advocate for Jews

Lazarus had never made any secret about her religion, and she had often written about Jewish themes. In the 1880s, the topic of Jews and their treatment by society became her principal theme, sparked in part by a wave of organized massacres—called "pogroms"—of Jews in southern Russia. For the last eight years of her life, Lazarus became one of the leading American writers on the subject of anti-Semitism and abuse of Jews. She wrote about the subject both in popular magazines and in publications read by Jews. Lazarus was among the first writers to urge Jews fleeing persecution in Europe to go to Palestine and establish a new Jewish nation on the site of ancient Israel. The idea of establishing a separate Jewish nation later came to be called Zionism and eventually resulted in the establishment of the modern state of Israel in 1947.

Lazarus also took direct action to help Jewish refugees. She visited camps set up for Jewish refugees on Ward's Island, in New York Harbor, and volunteered at the Hebrew Immigrant Aid Society, a group dedicated to assisting Jewish immigrants. Her writings led to the establishment of the Hebrew Technical Institute, designed to teach Jewish immigrants skills as mechanics. In 1883, she organized the Society for the Improvement and Colonization of East European Jews and tried to raise money from wealthy Jews in Europe to support it. After a year, the organization disbanded for lack of funds, however.

In 1883, in the midst of her work with Jews fleeing persecution in Russia, Lazarus submitted a poem as part of a fund-raising event designed to pay for the pedestal to be built under the Statue of Liberty. Earlier, France had announced that as a token of its friendship with the United States, it would donate a huge statue by sculptor Frédéric Auguste Bartholdi (1834–1904) to sit in New York Harbor, but it expected the United States to provide a base. The statue, which eventually became one of the most widely recognized symbols of the United States, was modeled after Bartholdi's mother (the face) and wife (the arms). In one arm, the tall figure of a woman held a tablet on which was engraved "1776," a reference to the year the Declaration of Independence, the document that de-

"The New Colossus"

> Not like the brazen giant of Greek fame,
> With conquering limbs astride from land to land;
> Here at our sea-washed, sunset gates shall stand
> A mighty woman with a torch, whose flame
> Is the imprisoned lightning, and her name
> Mother of Exiles. From her beacon-hand
> Glows world-wide welcome; her mild eyes command
> The air-bridged harbor that twin cities frame.
> "Keep ancient lands, your storied pomp!" cries she
> With silent lips. "Give me your tired, your poor,
> Your huddled masses yearning to breathe free,
> The wretched refuse of your teeming shore.
> Send these, the homeless, tempest-tost to me,
> I lift my lamp beside the golden door!"

—Emma Lazarus, 1883

clared that "all men are created equal," was signed and the United States became an independent republic ruled by the will of the people, overthrowing the rule of the British king. The other arm was holding a torch, symbolizing the freedom gained with the declaration of a republic. It was only later that the Statue of Liberty came to symbolize a beacon light for immigrants arriving from Europe.

The title of Lazarus's poem was "The New Colossus," and her reference to "the brazen giant of Greek fame, / With conquering limbs astride from land to land" recalled the Colossus of Rhodes, a statue built on the Mediterranean island

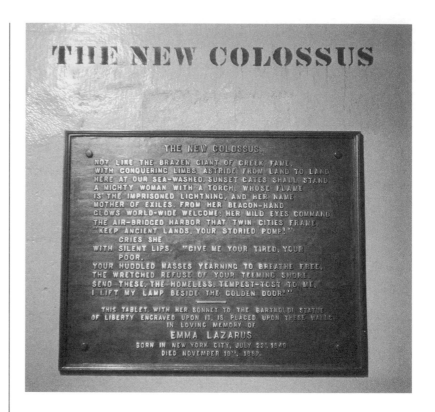

of Rhodes in 282 B.C.E. That statue of Helios, the Greek god of the sun, stood with one foot on either side of the entrance to the harbor of the island; its size made it one of the so-called ancient wonders of the world. (An earthquake brought down the original Colossus of Rhodes fifty-six years after its construction.) In mentioning the statue, Lazarus also meant to evoke the grandeur and ideals of ancient Greece, which included the democratic form of government, in which people vote for their leaders, while at the same time reminding the reader that this statue was a "new Colossus," symbolizing the break with the ancient world represented by the United States.

Lazarus wrote the poem at a time when she had become deeply involved with the plight of Jews in Europe affected by the Russian pogroms, which had touched off a wave of Jewish immigration to the United States. At about the same time, poor, landless peasants from Italy were also starting to arrive in New York, a southern European version of the flood of Irish immigrants of the late 1840s and 1850s. It was to these arriving immigrants that Lazarus referred when she wrote of "your poor, Your huddled masses yearning to breathe free, The wretched refuse of your teeming shore. Send these, the homeless, tempest-tost to me...."

Although her poem would later come to be associated with the Statue of Liberty, the association did not take place in Lazarus's lifetime. The statue was erected in 1886, just one year before Lazarus died, of cancer, at age thirty-eight. The poem lay forgotten until 1903, when the last five lines were engraved on a plaque and affixed to the statue's base.

With the addition of Lazarus's poem, the Statue of Liberty took on a new meaning. Rather than a monument to the republican form of government, as intended by its original French sponsor, it became a monument to the mass wave of migration that was, in 1903, delivering an unprecedented number of Europeans onto American shores. The poem symbolized for Americans and immigrants alike the image of the United States as a refuge.

That image of the United States was not to last. Beginning in 1921, the United States passed a series of laws that made it much harder for immigrants to enter the country. A 1924 law sharply reduced immigration from Europe by restricting the number of immigrants from southern and eastern Europe. The same concerns that had sparked the Know Nothing movement of the 1840s and 1850s had been renewed seventy years later.

—James L. Outman

For More Information

Books

Hayden, Richard S. *Restoring the Statue of Liberty: Sculpture, Structure, Symbol.* New York: McGraw-Hill, 1986.

Jacob, Heinrich Eduard. *The World of Emma Lazarus.* New York: Schocken Books, 1949.

Merriam, Eve. *Emma Lazarus, Woman with a Torch.* New York: Citadel Press, 1956.

Young, Bette Roth. *Emma Lazarus in Her World: Life and Letters.* Philadelphia: Jewish Publication Society, 1995.

Periodicals

Bodnar, John. "Symbols and Servants: Immigrant America and the Limits of Public History." *Journal of American History* (June 1986): p. 137.

Kleiger, Estelle F. "'I Lift My Lamp Beside the Golden Door!'" *American History Illustrated* (June 1986): p. 30.

Web Sites

"Emma Lazarus, 1849–1887." *Jewish Women's Archive.* http://www.jwa.org/exhibits/lazarus/el1.htm (accessed on March 18, 2004).

Lazarus, Emma. "The Poems of Emma Lazarus (Volume 1: Narrative, Lyric, and Dramatic)." *Project Gutenberg.* http://digital.library.upenn.edu/webbin/gutbook/lookup?num=3295 (accessed on March 18, 2004).

Bela Lugosi

Born October 20, 1882
Lugos, Hungary

Died August 16, 1956
Los Angeles, California

**Movie actor famous for
his roles in horror films**

"I am Count Dracula!"

Bela (pronounced BAY-la) Lugosi is arguably one of the most famous immigrants in film history. Although his career began on the stage in his native Hungary, he broke into films in the early 1930s in America when he accepted the choice role of Count Dracula for Universal Studios. Lugosi often shared the screen with the highly respected actor Boris Karloff (1887–1969) in his many horror films throughout the 1930s and into the 1940s, but he eventually took roles in lesser-quality movies, a career move that would prove his downfall. Per his will, Lugosi was buried in his Dracula cape.

Lugosi's career takes off

Bela Lugosi was born Béla Ferenc Dezsõ Blaskó on October 20, 1882, the youngest of four children in an upper-middle-class family. At twelve, Blaskó ran away from his small Hungarian hometown and survived by toiling in the mines and railroad yards. He never let go of his dream of becoming an actor, however, and he eventually landed a small role as a chorus boy in an operetta, an opera that is usually in the

Bela Lugosi. *Getty Images.*

251

form of a romantic comedy with songs and dancing. Through sheer determination and painstaking study, he eventually won larger roles that allowed him to travel throughout Hungary. Within a year, he had changed his name to Lugosi (meaning "one from Lugos," his hometown) and found himself in the desired position of leading actor in Hungary's Royal National Theatre.

Lugosi's roles were diverse and numerous. He appeared in as many as forty productions in one year, thanks largely in part to his singing ability, which gave him unusual flexibility. Lugosi had it all—good looks, acting ability, and vocal talent—and he used these qualities to his full advantage. His roles included Jesus Christ, Romeo, and a variety of others. In fact, it was his role as Romeo that brought him his greatest success at the time, and in 1911 he enjoyed unprecedented popularity in the capital city of Budapest.

Political turmoil sends actor to Germany and then America

After a short turn in the military during World War I (1914–18), Lugosi broke into films under the name Arisztid Olt. Although his acting career occupied much of his time, Lugosi had firm political beliefs and was deeply committed to change. After the collapse of the Hungarian monarchy, or royalty, and during the establishment of a communist regime in 1918, Lugosi worked tirelessly to organize an actors' union, an alliance of employees that works together to protect mutual benefits and rights. Communism is an economic theory characterized by a classless society in which goods are distributed equally, as compared with capitalism, which allows for competition and privately owned companies. The leftists, or liberal radicals in this case, who fought and spoke out against communism, were defeated a year later, however. This prompted Lugosi to flee to Germany, where he made another eleven films.

In 1921, Lugosi immigrated to America. In New York City, Lugosi established a Hungarian-language acting troupe and began to land character parts on stage and in films. The year 1923 would prove to be his breakthrough year in America. He scored the role of Fernando, the Spanish Apache, in the Broadway production of *The Red Poppy* as well as a notable role in the film *The Silent Command.* Unfortunately, Lugosi did not have a firm grasp of the English language, so he had to memorize his lines phonetically, which resulted in a very accented—and exotic—sound. His language difficulties resulted in a flop: the drama *The Right to Dream.* Lugosi signed on to direct the production in 1924 but found it impossible to communicate effectively with the cast and crew. The producers fired him; he sued. The courts found him unable to head a theatrical production and ordered him to pay a fine of nearly seventy dollars. Lugosi refused, and the contents of his apartment were auctioned off to satisfy his debt. This language barrier would continue to limit the quality of movies available to the multifaceted actor throughout his lifetime.

Dracula is born and Lugosi is saved

Just when it seemed the Hungarian actor would find no prosperity in America, he was hired to portray Count Dracula in the Broadway adaptation of Irish writer Bram Stoker's (1847–1912) vampire legend. Although Vlad Dracula (1431–1476) was a real human, Stoker's version of Dracula had little to do with the man. Vlad was a prince, born in Transylvania (ironically, a region just 50 miles from Lugosi's birthplace) and infamous for his brutality. His signature in battle was to leave his enemies impaled on wooden stakes (hence, Stoker's Dracula could be killed only with a wooden stake driven through the heart). Despite his reputation as a bloodthirsty warlord, he was revered by Romanians for his ruthless defense against the Turks in the invasions that marked the fifteenth century. Although the author's book was first published in 1897 and has never been out of print since, it only recently was published in Transylvania for a Romanian audience that generally does not appreciate the defamation, or injuring of a reputation through slander or the written word, of their national hero.

Lugosi played the role of Dracula on Broadway for one year, then took the production on the road for two more. Reviewers generally denounced the production as worthless; but theatergoers loved it. While performing in California, Lugosi attracted the attention of the major film studios and won himself supporting roles in several early talking films. Before the 1920s, most films were silent, that is, the actors did not speak (although during the showing of these films, music

Bela Lugosi in the horror film *Mark of the Vampire.* *Del Valle Archives.*

would be played in the theater by live musicians). The early talking pictures were not without flaws. There were problems with the amplification of sound, as technology was still in its infancy, and moviegoers often had trouble hearing the dialogue. In addition, because pictures and sound were recorded and played back using separate devices, synchronization was always an issue. In many instances, actors' lips would be moving, but the words were lagging behind.

U.S. Immigration and Migration: Biographies

In 1930, Universal Studios bought the rights to the Dracula story and began selecting the cast. The studio's first choice for the lead role was the legendary Lon Chaney Sr. (1883–1930). The actor was suffering from cancer, however, and would not live to play the evil aristocrat. Having lost his leading man even before filming began, director Tod Browning (1882–1962) began his search for a replacement. Having never agreed with Universal on a selection, he wanted an unknown to be cast as Dracula. When he could find no one suitable, he hired Lugosi at a low salary of $500 per week. The film—the first talking horror flick—was released in 1931 and sealed Lugosi's screen immortality; no one was more surprised than the actor and director when the movie became an instant megahit. Lugosi's opening line, "I am Dracula," delivered with a dark, brooding accent, remains one of the most widely imitated lines from a movie script. And those three words saved Lugosi's career as surely as they typecast him as a horror-genre actor.

Turns down Frankenstein

Having achieved instant international fame with his role as Dracula, Lugosi was immediately offered the starring role in *Frankenstein* directed by James Whale (1889–1957). In a poor business decision, Lugosi refused the offer in favor of playing the lead in a movie that never made it beyond the planning stages. The part was instead given to Boris Karloff (1887–1969), another horror actor whose ability to portray evil characters made him a screen legend.

Lugosi's refusal, based on the fact that Frankenstein had no speaking parts, harmed his reputation in the movie industry. Universal Studios did not appreciate Lugosi's arrogance in refusing to play Frankenstein, and top executives never forgot the actor's easy dismissal. As a result, his career seemed destined down the wrong path. Although Lugosi made dozens of films, some of them high-quality horror movies, many of them are forgettable, and he rarely earned more than $500 a week. He did not realize he was developing a reputation as a cheap actor, and he did not have the business sense to understand that he should have been paid much more than he was earning. Because he was not choosy in the roles he accepted, his box office value declined, and he was eternally downgrad-

The Dark Clark Gable

In his book on the subject of film stars of the horror genre, *Horror Film Stars,* author Michael Pitts shares some little-known information about Lugosi.

> *Unlike Lon Chaney Sr. and Boris Karloff, who projected their genre roles mainly through the grotesque (ugly, monstrous characters), Lugosi presented evil in well-mannered seductive ways, which certainly had an effect on the females of his audience. At one point in the mid-1930s, Lugosi received as much fan mail from female admirers as did handsome leading-man Clark Gable (1901–1960). This trend is doubly interesting since Lugosi worked mainly in horror films and at the time he was past fifty years of age.*

ed to act in B-grade movies. He did repeat his Dracula role in 1943 and again in 1948, at the age of sixty-six. Unfortunately, he eventually found himself playing bit parts in comedies that were nothing more than mere parodies, or takeoffs, of the character he made famous. Lugosi acknowledged his fate when he called himself "Dracula's puppet."

His most infamous role was in a movie directed by Ed Wood (1924–1978), *Plan 9 from Outer Space.* Wood was known in the movie industry for directing low-budget films, and *Plan 9* is considered by many diehard horror-movie fans as the worst movie ever made. Lugosi, featured in the film as a vampire, got top billing for the movie even though he died during production. He was replaced by Wood's wife's chiropractor (a therapist who performs spinal adjustments to improve a patient's health), who hid his face behind a cape for the rest of the movie. It was a sad ending to what could—and many say should—have been a glorious acting career.

Personal life tragic

Even during the higher points of Lugosi's career, his personal life was nothing less than tragic. When it came to marriage, Lugosi made poor choices, and his first three marriages dissolved before long. His fourth union, however, spanned two decades. Lugosi remained married to Lillian Arch for twenty years before she made the decision to leave the screen legend in 1953. Although they had a son, Bela Jr., life for the Lugosis was often overshadowed by financial concerns and the actor's addiction to morphine, a strong narcotic painkiller and sedative. He committed himself to the California State Hospital in 1955 to treat his addiction, but by then he had only a year to live. During this final year, he entered into his fifth marriage, this time with Hope Lininger, a loyal fan who had written letters to Lugosi every day while he was in the hospital.

As his career faltered, Lugosi became more eccentric. Earlier in his career, at the request of movie studios, he would appear in public in his vampire costume, and he even gave interviews from an open coffin. Later on, as his reputation became tarnished, he began going out in public in full costume of his own free will. His son has described the actor as a family man above all else, and indeed, his feelings for his fourth wife were passionate. Few people knew that Lugosi wrote poetry (from "My Darling Violetta," for instance: "Slumber envelops your beautiful face / And a dream grips your soul in embrace; / I will guard you"). Fewer still know that he studied modern sculpture.

Despite his personal and professional troubles, Lugosi remained active in political and civil causes. He was key in organizing the Screen Actors Guild in the mid-1930s, and he participated in fund-raising and morale-boosting efforts during World War II (1939–45).

Lugosi died of a heart attack at the age of seventy-three and was buried in full Dracula costume, including makeup and fangs, as requested in his will. He has since become something of a cult icon, and fans and actors alike remember him as a professional who, many believe, got much less than he deserved.

—*Rebecca Valentine*

For More Information

Books

Cremer, Robert. *Lugosi: The Man Behind the Cape*. Chicago: Henry Regenry, 1976.

Lennig, Arthur. *Immortal Count: The Life and Films of Bela Lugosi*. Lexington: University Press of Kentucky, 2003.

Pitts, Michael R. *Horror Film Stars*. Jefferson, NC: McFarland & Co., 1981.

Rhodes, Gary Don, and Richard Sheffield. *Lugosi: His Life in Films, on Stage, and in the Hearts of Horror Lovers*. Jefferson, NC: McFarland, 1997.

Web Sites

"Bela Lugosi." *Brian's Drive-In Theater*. http://www.briansdriveintheater.com/belalugosi.html (accessed on March 22, 2004).

"Dear Old Pals." *Winter Steel*. http://www.wintersteel.homestead.com/files/JamesArticles/Karloff_and_Lugosi.htm (accessed on March 22, 2004).

Tournier, Johanne L. "Bela Bio for Flatt World." *The Webworld of Bela Lugosi*. http://users.auracom.com/tournier/flattworldbio.htm (accessed on March 22, 2004).

Daniel Patrick Moynihan

Born March 6, 1927
Tulsa, Oklahoma

Died March 26, 2003
Washington, D.C.

Social scientist and U.S. senator

D aniel Patrick Moynihan had two careers: the first as a professor and sociologist, and the second as a public servant and U.S. senator from New York. As a sociologist, Moynihan created a stir in 1963 when he and coauthor Nathan Glazer (1923–) published *Beyond the Melting Pot: The Negroes, Puerto Ricans, Jews, Italians, and Irish of New York City,* challenging the idea that as different nationalities came to the United States, they melded together to create a new "American" identity.

As a politician, Moynihan was a Democrat, but he held positions under both Democratic and Republican presidents. He often used his academic work in trying to solve difficult social problems, such as the endurance of poverty among African Americans. As a result, Moynihan was difficult to pin down as a conservative or a liberal. A conservative has a political philosophy of limited government influence and supports conventional social values. A liberal is someone who favors active government influence and is more open to new ideas and individual rights.

"Religion and race define the next stage in the evolution of the American peoples."

Daniel Patrick Moynihan.
Getty Images.

259

Early life in New York

Moynihan's best known academic work was about New York City, where Moynihan spent much of his childhood. He was born, however, far from New York: in Tulsa, Oklahoma, where his father, John Henry Moynihan, was a journalist and his mother, Margaret Ann Phipps, was a painter and sculptor. His father moved his family, which in addition to Daniel Patrick included a younger brother and a sister, from job to job, sometimes working in advertising. In 1937, Moynihan's father abandoned the family.

The sudden disappearance of Moynihan's father forced his mother to scramble to earn a living. She and her children moved from a middle-class suburb into Manhattan's Hell's Kitchen, a rough neighborhood near the docks of the Hudson River. As a boy, Moynihan sometimes shined shoes in Times Square to earn money. Later, he worked unloading and loading ships. His mother at one point owned a bar, where Moynihan also worked occasionally.

Living and working in Manhattan gave Moynihan a very different perspective on American society than he might have gotten had his family remained in a city like Tulsa. For one thing, New York had a much greater variety of ethnic groups, or people who maintained their sense of being part of a group of people who had emigrated from a particular country in Europe, than most Midwestern or southern cities. New York in the 1930s and 1940s remained largely a city of immigrants; as late as 1960, half the city's population had been born outside the United States.

Moynihan attended a variety of schools in New York, both Catholic and public, and graduated from Benjamin Franklin High School. He started attending City College of New York, and after a year joined the Navy Reserve, which sent him to Middlebury College in Vermont for a year to train as an officer, and then to Tufts University near Boston, Massachusetts, where Moynihan earned both a bachelor's and a master's degree in 1949. Moynihan started working on a doctorate in sociology, but he did not finish his doctoral degree (Ph.D.) until 1961.

Moynihan as public servant

After first serving in the military, which had financed his college education, Moynihan began what proved to be a

The Melting Pot

"The Melting Pot" is a phrase borrowed from a play of the same name by an English playwright, Israel Zangwill (1864–1926). The play, which was a hit in New York when it opened in 1908, is about the coming together of various nationalities in the United States—in the form of a love story. U.S. president Theodore Roosevelt (1858–1919; served 1901–9) was said to have loved the play when he saw it, shouting to the author, "Bully, Mr. Zangwill! Bully!"—an expression of the time meaning excellent or first rate.

Long after Zangwill's play was forgotten, the image persisted of the United States as a place where old hostilities and differences that separated emigrants when they lived in Europe would disappear. The expression "melting pot" was taken from industrial processing: the image was of different types of metal being poured into a pot, where they would melt (in the heat of passion in the case of Zangwill's play) and come together as an alloy, a kind of new metal that would be superior to any of the individual ingredients. The key notion was that different nationalities would enter the United States and merge into a new nationality: the American.

The sentiment was especially popular with Jewish immigrants in the United States, who had long been excluded from full participation in the European societies from which they came. In the United States, freedom to practice one's own religion was guaranteed and discrimination based on religion was to be banned. It was also an idea popularly taught in public schools for most of the twentieth century as part of an effort by the government to avoid conflicts between immigrant groups and to promote national unity, especially when the United States found itself going to war against the very countries (such as Italy) which had been home to many immigrants or their immediate ancestors.

half-century career that mixed politics with academics. In the mid-1950s Moynihan plunged into the politics of New York City, which with a population of about seven million was the nation's largest city. It was also traditionally the major point of entry for immigrants of all sorts. In the 1950s, the city had large populations of African Americans, who had come (or whose parents had come) from the American South, as well as Puerto Ricans from the U.S. territory in the Caribbean. In politics, Irish Americans often competed with Jewish Americans for dominance in city government.

Moynihan began his political career as a volunteer in the New York City mayoral campaign of Robert F. Wagner Jr.

Israel Zangwill, the playwright who popularized the phrase "melting pot" to describe the mixing of cultures between immigrants in the United States. *Hulton-Deutsch Collection/Bettmann-Corbis.*

(1910–1991) in 1953. The experience was important since New York City politics was strongly influenced by the various national groups that still lived in the same neighborhoods of the city, much as they had when their ancestors arrived from Europe.

Moynihan worked for New York governor Averill Harriman (1891–1986) from 1955 to 1958, during which time he attracted notice with a study of automobile accidents. Whereas most studies of car accidents treated the subject as one related to driving and focused on safer cars and better highway design, Moynihan viewed car accidents as a public health problem that involved issues far removed from cars and highways, issues like alcohol, exhaustion, and social stress. Moynihan then worked for the New York State Democratic Committee for two years, and was a delegate to the Democratic convention in 1960. The convention saw the nomination of U.S. senator John F. Kennedy (1917–1963) of Massachusetts, who became the first Catholic of Irish ancestry to be elected president.

In 1959, Moynihan started work as director of a New York state government research project at Syracuse University, where he later was also an assistant professor of political science for two years (1961–62). With the election of Kennedy, Moynihan moved to Washington, D.C., where he worked as an assistant to the secretary of labor from 1961 to 1963. Moynihan tried his hand at electoral politics, running (but losing) in the party primary for president of the New York City Council in 1965. He then worked for the mayoral campaign of Abraham Beame (1906–2001) in 1965.

The next year he taught at Wesley University, then moved to Cambridge, Massachusetts, to teach at the Joint Center for Urban Studies run by Harvard University and the Massachusetts Institute of Technology, where he stayed until 1977. During this period, he was also a professor of government at Harvard and was appointed to several key posts in the administration of President Richard Nixon (1913–1994; served 1969–74). These positions included counselor to the president and executive secretary of Urban Affairs Council (1969–70), ambassador to India (1973–75), and U.S. ambassador to the United Nations (1975–76).

Beyond the Melting Pot

Although Moynihan wrote extensively, the work that brought him to fame initially was *Beyond the Melting Pot,* written with his fellow professor Nathan Glazer (1923–) and published in 1963. The book's subtitle was *The Negroes, Puerto Ricans, Jews, Italians, and Irish of New York City.* Moynihan and Glazer studied the habits and attitudes of five of New York's largest groups and concluded that "the point about the melting pot … is that it did not happen." Instead, members of national groups have continued to identify themselves as belonging to a group within American society. This attitude, expressed as "I'm Irish" or "I'm Italian," showed up in many different ways in New York: in where people lived in the city, what jobs they held, what food they ate, and the people with whom they associated.

The authors found nothing surprising in the persistence of national identities. Rather than fading over time, they discovered that national identities sometimes grew stronger with succeeding generations. Although the children of immigrants might have once felt embarrassed about the "old country" ways of their parents, the grandchildren and great-grandchildren of immigrants often felt just the opposite: proud to be "Irish," or "Italian," even if they had never visited their ancestral land and could not speak the language of their ancestral land.

The Moynihan-Glazer study found that such attitudes were not shared by all ethnic groups. Descendants from the earliest English settlers, for example, did not think of themselves as anything but Americans. Many descendants of German immigrants no longer identified with their ancestral land, partly because German immigrants had shared many traits with the English settlers who preceded them and partly because Germany's roles in World War I (1914–18) and World War II

U.S. senator Daniel Patrick Moynihan of New York makes a point during a speech. *AP/Wide World Photos.*

(1939–45), when the United States and Germany fought one another, may have diminished the inclination to loudly identify with a country perceived to have started both conflicts.

For many other nationalities, however, "ethnicity is more than an influence on events," the authors concluded. "It is commonly the source of events. Social and political institutions do not merely respond to ethnic interests; a great number of institutions exist for the specific purpose of serving ethnic interests. This in turn tends to perpetuate them."

Moynihan and Glazer identified two other aspects of a person's identity that also served to keep apart different groups of Americans: race and religion. They noted, for example, that among African Americans, Protestant clergymen often played a prominent role in the politics of the black community, which would be extremely rare among Catholics. "Racc and religion," they wrote, "define the next stage in the evolution of the American peoples. But the American nationality is still forming: Its processes are mysterious, and the final form, if there is ever to be a final form, is as yet unknown."

Senator Moynihan

In his role as presidential advisor, Moynihan continued to bring the sensibility of a professor to government. Many politicians tended to assess government policy in terms of how it might impact the economic well-being of different groups, but Moynihan made a reputation as someone who wanted to study facts before reaching any conclusions about how government could best help individuals or groups of individuals. In the case of African Americans, for example, Moynihan concluded that racial discrimination might not be the most important reason for the persistent poverty that plagues black people in America. He suggested instead that the breakdown in African American families (for example, the high frequency of single-parent families) might be a more important reason that black Americans have, overall, not kept pace economically with whites. Such views did not always make Moynihan popular among his fellow Democrats, especially when they were expressed as an advisor to Republican presidents like Richard Nixon.

In 1976, Moynihan was elected to the Senate, representing New York, where he remained for the next twenty-four years. Just as he had done as a professor and advisor to presidents, Moynihan continued to urge innovative solutions to social problems, based on close study of the facts rather than on standard political philosophy.

Moynihan retired from the Senate in 2000 and returned to Syracuse University to teach. First lady Hillary Rodham Clinton (1947–) succeeded Moynihan following her victory in the November election. Moynihan died in March 2003.

—*James L. Outman*

For More Information

Books

Glazer, Nathan, and Daniel Patrick Moynihan. *Beyond the Melting Pot: The Negroes, Puerto Ricans, Jews, Italians, and Irish of New York City.* Cambridge, MA: MIT Press and Harvard University Press, 1962.

Glazer, Nathan, and Daniel P. Moynihan, eds. *Ethnicity: Theory and Experience.* Cambridge, MA: Harvard University Press, 1975.

Hodgson, Godfrey. *The Gentleman from New York: Daniel Patrick Moynihan, a Biography.* Boston: Houghton Mifflin, 2000.

Katzmann, Robert A., ed. *Daniel Patrick Moynihan: The Intellectual in Public Life.* Washington, DC: The Woodrow Wilson Center Press, 1998.

Moynihan, Daniel P. *Loyalties.* New York: Harcourt Brace Jovanovich, 1984.

Schoen, Douglas E. *Pat: A Biography of Daniel Patrick Moynihan.* New York: Harper and Row, 1979.

Periodicals

Alter, Jonathan. "A Man of Ideas in the Arena: Sen. Daniel Patrick Moynihan, 1927–2003." *Newsweek* (April 7, 2003): p. 63.

Heilbrunn, Jacob. "The Moynihan Enigma." *The American Prospect* (July-August 1997): p. 18.

Nuechterlein, James. "The Moynihan Years." *Commentary* (October 2000): p. 29.

Roberts, Sam. "Melting Pot: A Look Back and Beyond." *New York Times* (May 17, 1990): p. A24.

Web Sites

"Moynihan, Daniel Patrick, 1927–2003." *Congressional Biography.* http://bioguide.congress.gov/scripts/biodisplay.pl?index=M001054 (accessed on March 21, 2004).

Josie Natori

Born May 9, 1947
Manila, Philippines

Chief executive officer of a leading clothes and fashion accessories firm

Josie Natori has been an immensely successful business-woman in the diverse fields of investment banking and fashion. Natori made a major change in her life at the age of thirty—leaving the security of a high-paying position in banking to start a business, the Natori Company, importing crafts and clothes from the Philippines. Acting on a comment by a purchase agent, one who selects clothes that a store will sell, that a blouse Natori was selling would be more attractive as a nightshirt, Natori started a line of women's clothes that can be worn as intimate apparel or high fashion, as sleepwear or outer garments. Founded in 1977 and still thriving over twenty-five years later, the Natori Company has annual sales that exceed $50 million.

"Respect yourself and your vocation. Respect is the result of passion. You cannot expect to get respectful reactions from people if what you are doing doesn't originate from deep within your soul."

Family influences

Born Josefina Almeda Cruz in Manila, Philippines, on May 9, 1947, Natori was the eldest of six children. Her father, Felipe, owned a construction company and was an entrepreneur, one who invests in people with ideas for new business

Josie Natori, second from left, with models. *James Keyser/Time Life Pictures/Getty Images.*

ventures and inventions. Her mother, Angelita Cruz, was trained as a pharmacist, but she also worked as her husband's business partner. Natori's maternal grandmother, Josefa Almeda, a hard-working and fiercely independent businesswoman, became a role model for Natori. She lived with the family and helped maintain a strict, Catholic upbringing for the children.

Natori's mother had an artistic side, playing piano and collecting works of art. She encouraged her daughter when Natori began playing the piano at age four. Natori became so accomplished that she played as a piano soloist with the Manila Philharmonic Orchestra at age nine. She attended Catholic schools in Manila, and as a high-school graduation gift, she went on a world-travel tour with her mother.

Natori remained for a time in Paris, and then New York City, where she decided she wanted to live. She enrolled in Manhattanville College in 1964 to study economics. Natori graduated in 1968 and began working as an investment banker with Bache Securities. Quickly making a strong impression, Natori opened a company office in Manila. She was able to attract Filipino businesspeople and investors to work with Bache, and then returned to New York.

Natori moved to Merrill Lynch, another investment banking firm. She was made a vice president of the firm by the time she reached the age of twenty-seven in 1974. Meanwhile, Natori had met her future husband, Kenneth Natori, on a blind date. He also worked on Wall Street (the major financial district of the United States, located in New York City), where he was an investment banker for Shearson Lehman Brothers, a rival firm. The Natoris were married in 1972, and in 1976 their son, Kenneth Jr., was born.

Daring to change

By 1977, Natori had accomplished everything she had wanted to in the field of finance. She and her husband wanted to start a business and considered buying a franchise outlet for fast food or clothes cleaning. But Natori saw an exciting opportunity in finely crafted items from the Philippines, which Natori believed would spark interest in the United States. She founded the Natori Company to import and sell items ranging from furniture to clothes. When Natori received a finely embroidered blouse from a friend as an example of Philippine-made clothes she could sell in her business, she seized the opportunity. "I knew there was a niche [market spot] for that," she told *Nation's Business.*

Natori soon showed she had an ear, as well as an eye, for items that would sell well. A buyer, or agent who purchases items to sell, at Bloomingdales' Department Store in New York City suggested that Natori lengthen the blouse and turn it into a nightshirt women could wear at home. Natori took the buyer's suggestion. Soon after, the first order came in for one thousand nightshirts. Natori quit investment banking to devote her full attention to the Natori Company. That was in the spring of 1977. By summer, Natori had designed a line of sleepwear using Philippine fabrics and detail work. Before winter came, she had $150,000 worth of orders.

"Respect yourself and your vocation," Natori would tell *Entrepreneur* magazine twenty-years later in an article titled "Tip Sheet: Top Entrepreneurs Share Their Hottest Sales Pointers." She explained how changing her career renewed her energy: "I began building an image because I was on fire from within. I was doing what I wanted to do again. For many years, I felt that way on Wall Street, but when the feelings were no longer there, I left. The reason many salespeople no longer get respect from their clients is that they no longer respect what they do or themselves for doing it. Always use your inner life as your guide to building a respectable image."

Despite not even knowing how to sew, Natori was the guiding creative force for the company's line of upscale lingerie or women's underwear. Since she had no formal design training, she hired an independent designer to turn her ideas into material reality. A businesswoman first and foremost, Natori began to participate in the fashion world, from meeting with buyers to having her line of clothes shown by models on runway exhibits in Paris and New York. In the early years of the Natori Company, she often used her New York and Paris apartments as showrooms of new fashions to prospective buyers. She flew to Manila to oversee production and to ensure that clothes were cut to specific sizes and specifications. Maintaining quality was a challenge because Natori was relying on managers and groups of workers she had only recently begun to employ.

A family affair

Natori depended on friends and relatives for help—an uncle pitched in to sew labels on to clothes during breaks from his job as a surgeon, and family members gathered to make a small trim cut on each item for a special order of one thousand blouses. In 1979, the company was better able to control quality and production by building its own sewing factory in the Philippines. The factory was built and operated by Natori's father.

The Natori Company quickly became famous for clothes that reflect the designs and craftsmanship of the Philippines as well as Asian themes and materials, including silk, crocodile leather, suede, black resin, and fabrics used in kimonos, traditional Japanese robes. By 1985, her company was so successful that Natori needed help in balancing her role as chief executive officer with her hands-on work in design, sales, marketing, and production. She persuaded her husband, Ken Natori, to leave his high-paying executive position on Wall Street to join the firm. He became chairman of the Natori Company.

The flourishing business created job opportunities in the Philippines. For helping the Filipino economy and displaying to the world the excellent craftsmanship of Filipino workers, Natori was honored in 1988 with the Galleon Award by Corazon Aquino (1933–), who was then president of the Philippines. Drawing on her cultural heritage for inspiration, Natori noted in a *Women's Wear Daily* profile that "the whole trademark of Natori is based on craftsmanship out of the Philippines. I took the best of what I am about, and combined it in this business."

New challenges

Always looking for new opportunities, the Natori Company consistently expanded its line of items during the 1990s. In addition to lingerie, Natori developed stylish pajamas, robes, pants, and tank tops in a wide variety of fabrics. In 1991, the company introduced Josie Natori Couture, a collection of elegant evening wear and dresses. A fashion jewelry collection was released in the fall of 1993, and in 1994 a day and evening shoe collection. Fragrances, including the perfumes *Josie* and *Natori,* were introduced in 1995.

The company continued prospering, in fact, because it was willing to change by responding to trends and sometimes influencing them. To keep on the front line of the fashion industry, Natori worked tirelessly, traveling to different places in the world two to four times a month and being the face of the company—the person most closely identified with what the company offers. Such a life requires much travel, many quick meals and meetings, daily discussion of new ideas, and quick decision-making. Barely over 5 feet tall and weighing less than 100 pounds, Natori is a powerhouse of energy.

She divided the Natori label into two different entities for different kinds of women: the Natori Black label appeals to women who prefer elegant and luxurious silk and lace clothes, while the Natori White Label is intended for women who prefer modern casual styles. In 1998, she repositioned the Josie label to emphasize more contemporary fashion prints and colors, and the Cruz line to focus on more mainstream consumers.

A selection of scarves was introduced in 1999, and in 2001 handbags were added to accessories offered by the Natori Company. Reflecting how Natori reacts to challenges and opportunities, the handbag line quickly became the best-selling accessory item even though it was the one most recently introduced. A collection of belts was released in 2002. By then, the Natori Company was consistently generating over $40 million in annual sales.

For her efforts and successes, Natori won numerous awards. In 1999, she was named number forty in the Goldsea 100, America's 100 Top Asian Entrepreneurs list. Natori was awarded the Ellis Island Medal of Honor for distinguished achievement by an American immigrant. Working with the administration of President Bill Clinton (1946–; served 1993–2001), she served as a delegate to the Economic Summit Conference in Little Rock, Arkansas, in 1992, and as a commissioner to the White House Conference on Small Business in 1993. An advocate for women's rights, she received the National Organization of Women (NOW) Legal Defense and Education Fund Buddy award in 1990. In 1998, Natori was chosen as the New York City Partnership's Business Woman of the Year. In 2000, Natori worked with the Asia Society to direct an exhibition in New York City by up-and-coming designers inspired by Philippine tradition.

Summing up the success of the Natori Company in 2002, *Womens' Wear Daily* noted that the Natoris managed to continually grow and prosper "in an industry battered by a frenzy of bankruptcies and mergers and acquisitions. Their longevity comes from an astute sense of business acumen [intelligence] combined with a personal warmth that has charmed and disarmed supporters as well as competitors."

—Roger Matuz

For More Information

Books

Bautista, Veltisezar. *The Filipino Americans (from 1763 to the Present): Their History, Culture and Traditions.* Midlothian, VA: Bookhaus Publishers, 1998.

Crisostomo, Isabelo T. *Filipino Achievers in the USA & Canada.* Midlothian, VA: Bookhaus Publishers, 1996.

Kim, Hyung-Chan, ed. *Distinguished Asian Americans: A Biographical Dictionary.* Westport, CT: Greenwood Publishing Group, 1999.

Periodicals

Monget, Karyn, and Kletter, Melanie. "Natori's 25 Year Mystique." *Women's Wear Daily* (November 25, 2002): p. 6.

Willen, Janet A. "Fashioning a Business." *Nation's Business* (February 1995): p. 14.

Web Sites

"Asia Society Presents Philippine Style 2000." *Asia Society.* http://www.asiasociety.org/pressroom/rel-newsphilstyle.html (accessed on March 22, 2004).

"Josie Natori." *Natori.* http://www.natori.com/pages/natori-designer.html (accessed on March 22, 2004).

"Top Entrepreneurs Share Their Hottest Sales Pointers." *Entrepreneur* (June 1998). http://www.entrepreneur.com/mag/article/0,1539, 228838,00.html (accessed on March 22, 2004).

Yoko Ono

Born February 18, 1933
Tokyo, Japan

Artist, writer, and performer

When Yoko Ono turned seventy in 2003, she was enjoying more popular and critical respect than at any time during her more than forty years as an artist. A large retrospective exhibit of her artwork, called Transmodern Yoko, was on a world tour. Songs she released twenty years earlier had been remixed by contemporary artists and were playing regularly at dance clubs. "People think that their world will get smaller as they get older," she told Steve Dougherty of *People* magazine. "My experience is just the opposite. Your senses become more acute. You start to blossom."

Her career began with a small art-crowd following interested in her experimental art, films, and music. Then, Ono became internationally famous for her romance with John Lennon (1940–1980), a member of the the Beatles, the best-selling and most popular musical group of the 1960s. When the Beatles broke up in 1970, Ono was seen by some as having been a divisive force that contributed to Lennon's dissatisfaction with the band as well as having a negative impact on his music. After John and Yoko (as they were best known) turned to a quiet home life in the mid-1970s to raise their

"When I first came out there was a lot of xenophobia [fear of foreigners] and suspicion because I was an Oriental woman standing with John [Lennon]. It scared people, and I understood that in some way. Now I'm 70, and people could say 'She's old' and be intolerant, but they haven't…. It's nice not to feel like an outsider. It's opened my life up."

Yoko Ono. © *Michael S. Yamashita/Corbis.*

son, Sean (1975–), they reemerged in 1980 with a hit album, *Double Fantasy*. But Lennon was murdered in December of that year. Since then, Ono reemerged as an artist in her own right and helped keep alive the spirit of peace and imagination she and Lennon had found.

Art as event

Yoko Ono (whose name means "Ocean Child" in Japanese) was born into a wealthy family on February 18, 1933, in Tokyo, Japan. Her father, Eisuke (1935–), was head of the Bank of Japan. Her mother, Isoko, was from one of the richest and most powerful families in Japan. Her father, who had wanted to be a concert pianist, encouraged Ono's early interest in music, but his insistence in directing her actually contributed to her rebellion against "acceptable" music. Ono went to the Gakushuin School, which was usually reserved for members of Japan's royal family. When she was seven, her family moved briefly to Long Island, New York. They soon returned to Japan just before America entered World War II (1939–45) following the Japanese attack on Pearl Harbor, Hawaii, in December 1941.

As World War II progressed, American planes began bombing Tokyo. The Ono children had an opportunity to stay in the Royal Palace with Ono's friends from school. Instead, their mother took them to a country home she had commissioned to be built. The house turned out to be poorly constructed, and the family had meager provisions while living in wartime conditions. Following the end of World War II, the family returned to Tokyo and Ono finished school. In her musical studies, she became greatly interested in vocal arrangements. Ono briefly attended Gakushuin University in Tokyo, where she was the first female student to focus on philosophy.

After she moved with her family to Scarsdale, a wealthy New York suburb, in 1951, Ono attended Sarah Lawrence College. She studied music, becoming fascinated with experiments in tone, and began writing poetry. She dropped out of college in 1955 to focus on her art. Ono met Toshi Ichiyanagi (1933–), an avant-garde, or unconventional, pianist who had been a student of John Cage (1912–1992), a leading composer whose work incorporated disorder, use of everyday noises, and randomness. The couple married in 1957 and moved to Manhattan. In 1958, Ono began showing her conceptual art pieces, in which the audience or viewer of the art contributed to the piece.

Ono's loft in Greenwich Village became a performance space by the early 1960s. In addition to displaying her conceptual art, she hosted "events" organized by composer La Monte Young (1935–). Young was part of a movement called "Fluxus" that attempted to break free from conventional standards of art and music. In 1961, Ono gave her first public musical performance. Held at the Village Gate in New York, the performance featured mumbled words, laughter, atonal music, and an actor speaking in monotone, according to Barbara Haskell in an essay that appeared in the catalogue, or guide, to Ono's later exhibit in 1989 at the Whitney Museum.

In 1963, Ono and Ichiyanagi lived briefly in Japan before breaking up and divorcing. Ono married avant-garde artist and filmmaker Tony Cox in 1964. They had a child, Kyoko. Also in that year, she published *Grapefruit,* a collection of surrealist poems and meditations. (Surrealism is a style of art and literature in which the artist or writer produces fantastic or other-worldly images by using unnatural or unusual combinations of elements.) John Lennon would say later that *Grapefruit* inspired his famous song, "Imagine" (one line from "Tunafish Sandwich Piece" is "Imagine one thousand suns in the sky at the same time").

In 1966, Ono was invited to participate in a multimedia conference/show in London called the "Destruction in Art Symposium." She and Cox traveled often to London, Paris, and New York between 1964 and 1968. They collaborated on a series of films while in London, including *Bottoms* (1967), which consists of close-ups of 365 bare backsides. In Paris, Ono met jazz saxophonist Ornette Coleman (1930–), who further stimulated her interest in vocal experimentation. Her songs, according to Kristine McKenna in the *Los Angeles Times,* blended inspirations from experimental operettas, Japanese Kabuki (stylized theatrical) singing called *hetai,* Indian and Tibetan vocal techniques, and freejazz. "Ono synthesized those elements into sound collages that had no precedent and haven't been matched yet in sheer adventurousness," wrote McKenna. Many of these pieces were collected in *Onobox,* a

John Lennon and Yoko Ono at an art exhibition in Syracuse, New York, in October 1971. *Corbis-Bettmann.*

six-CD collection of Ono's solo musical work released in 1992. Some of the pieces are from a series of events she performed at Carnegie Recital Hall during this period.

Meets the Beatle

Having returned to London in 1968, Ono exhibited her artwork at Indica Gallery. The works included *Painting to Hammer Nail In.* It consisted of a wood panel with a hammer attached, which viewers were encouraged to use to pound nails into the panel—an example of her art that invited audience participation. John Lennon visited the exhibition and met Ono for the first time. Both were married at the time to other people, but they began seeing each other. After both divorced their spouses, Lennon and Ono were married on March 20, 1969.

Lennon was still with the Beatles, but the band members by this time were involved in various projects and often

U.S. Immigration and Migration: Biographies

recorded separately. Fans hopeful that the Beatles would stay together blamed Ono, who accompanied Lennon everywhere, for Lennon's growing disinterest in the band. She sat in and sometimes contributed to recording sessions. But Lennon already had plans to move on from the band, and group infighting had led the band's drummer, Ringo Starr (1940–), to consider leaving as well.

Ono and Lennon, meanwhile, celebrated their relationship publicly. They staged an open honeymoon in Paris and Amsterdam and Lennon wrote a song about it that was one of the last Beatle recordings, "The Ballad of John and Yoko." In the spring of 1969, they staged a "bed-in" in Toronto, Ontario, Canada, where celebrities and reporters crowded around the couple in bed in a hotel room. They announced they were promoting world peace, especially an end to the Vietnam War (1954–75). Lennon's song "Give Peace a Chance," recorded at the "bed-in," became a hit single and an anthem, or theme song, for peace activists, who sang the chorus, "All we are saying / is give peace a chance," at antiwar demonstrations.

Ono and Lennon began collaborating on songs, but most fans of Lennon would not accept her as a legitimate contributor. She signed with Apple Records, a label founded by the Beatles, and continued recording her vocal experimentations. In 1970, Ono and Lennon released individual albums, both titled *Plastic Ono Band,* but her album received poor reviews and sparked little public interest. Her next album, *Fly,* showed the influence of her involvement in primal scream therapy.

Contentment and tragedy
The couple briefly separated in 1974, but soon reunited and had a son, Sean, who was born in 1975 on his father's birthday. Lennon and Ono stayed out of the public eye for much of the rest of the decade. Lennon focused on raising his son, and Ono managed the family's extensive financial holdings—the Beatles had been the best-selling band in the history of recorded music. Ono revealed great business know-how as an investor in art, real estate, and cattle, and built up the

family fortune estimated somewhere between $500 million and $1 billion.

Ono and Lennon returned to the recording studio and released the album *Double Fantasy* in 1980. More relaxed and melodic than their previous albums, *Double Fantasy* was popular and warmly received. It features seven compositions by Ono and seven by Lennon. Shortly after the album was released, Lennon was returning to his New York apartment after a recording session on a new song by Ono called "Walking on Thin Ice." Lennon was gunned down by Mark David Chapman (1955–), a psychotic "fan" outside the apartment building. Fans around the world were stunned that a man who had sung about peace and love was brutally murdered.

Ono and her son Sean neither avoided nor contributed to the international attention surrounding the killing, with the exception of making grateful acknowledgements to mourners. Ono gradually released new material that included Lennon songs, images of him on film, and his writings over the next decade. Meanwhile, she gradually returned to the public that had once been so critical of her influence on Lennon.

In 1981, Ono released an album, *Season of Glass,* that ignited some controversy for its cover, which showed the blood-stained broken pair of eyeglasses Lennon was wearing when he was killed, and for a song that consisted of gunshots followed by wailing. In a *New York Times* article of August 5, 1981, Ono stated, "What was I supposed to do, avoid the subject? … A lot of people advised me that I shouldn't put that on the cover of the record, but I wanted the whole world to see those glasses with blood on them and to realize that John had been *killed*. It wasn't like he died of old age or drugs or something." A highlight of the album was "Walking on Thin Ice," the song she had been recording on the night Lennon was killed. The song earned Ono a Grammy Award nomination.

Ono became active in various musical, film, and artistic pursuits. In 1984, she released the album *Milk and Honey,* which included new songs as well as several songs recorded by Lennon that were previously unreleased. Ono produced the movie and soundtrack for *Imagine* in 1988, which blended scenes from her other film projects, home movies, and new songs. In 1989, the Whitney Museum of American Art in

New York staged a retrospective of her work from the 1960s, and the Museum of Modern Art showed several of her films, along with those by other Fluxus artists. Another retrospective in 2002, Transmodern Yoko, showed art spanning her entire career. After making its debut at New York's Japan Society Gallery, the exhibit went on a world tour.

The collection *Onobox,* a 1992 musical retrospective of Ono's solo work, received acclaim that had been minimal when many of the songs were first released. "That she made music of marginal worth is repudiated [rejected] once and for all by this lavish, illuminating six-CD overview of her remarkable pop life," wrote David Fricke in *Rolling Stone* magazine. In 1994, Ono created *New York Rock,* an opera for the WPA Theater in New York City.

Ono's seventieth birthday in 2003 drew wide attention in the media. The popularity of remixes of her songs at dance clubs made Ono a performer in demand again, noted Josh Tyrangiel in *Time* magazine. She does not attempt to hide her pleasure at her unexpected relevance, he noted. "I think it's a message," she said to Tyrangiel. "When I first came out there was a lot of xenophobia [fear of foreigners] and suspicion because I was an Oriental woman standing with John. It scared people, and I understood that in some way. Now I'm 70, and people could say 'She's old' and be intolerant, but they haven't. This club world has been so embracing. It's nice not to feel like an outsider. It's opened my life up."

—*Roger Matuz*

For More Information

Books

Haskell, Barbara. "Yoko Ono: Objects." In *Yoko Ono: Objects, Films.* New York: The Whitney Museum of American Art, 1989.

Hendricks, Jon, ed. *YES Yoko Ono* (book and CD). New York: Harry N. Abrams, 2001.

Sheff, David. *All We Are Saying: The Last Major Interview with John Lennon and Yoko Ono.* New York: Griffin Trade Paperback, 2000.

Periodicals

Dougherty, Steve. "Oh Yes! Ono Turns 70: Yoko Ono Finds Happiness in Her Kids, Her Art and Memories of John." *People* (March 31, 2003): pp. 97–103.

Fricke, David. "Onobox." *Rolling Stone* (March 19, 1992).

Mahoney, J. W. "Transmodern Yoko." *Art in America* (February 2002).

McKenna, Kristine. "Yoko Reconsidered." *Los Angeles Times* (April 11, 1993): p. CAL3.

Palmer, Robert. "Yoko Ono Asks: 'Was I Supposed to Avoid the Subject?'" *New York Times* (August 5, 1981): p. C17.

Perreault, John. "Yoko Ono at the Whitney: Age of Bronze." *Village Voice* (February 7, 1989): p. 29.

Tyrangiel, Josh. "An Unlikely Dance Queen: Twenty-two Years after Its Release, a Dusty Yoko Ono Song Becomes a Dance-club Chart Topper." *Time* (May 26, 2003): p. 71.

Web Sites

AIU: A Yoko Ono Box. http://www.a-i-u.net/ (accessed on March 22, 2004).

Instant Karma! A John and Yoko Site. http://www.instantkarma.com/ (accessed on March 22, 2004).

Onoweb. http://www.jeclique.com/onoweb/ (accessed on March 22, 2004).

I. M. Pei

Born April 26, 1917
Canton (now Guangzhou), China

Architect famous for designing museums and other structures

When I. M. Pei retired from full-time work in the 1990s, he was one of the most famous architects of the twentieth century. His building designs feature simple, geometrical forms, like triangles and rectangles. These forms take on dramatic flourishes in Pei's buildings by his use of glass walls, distinctively colored stone, and other eye-catching materials. Pei approaches each project as a unique opportunity to match the look of the building with the purpose for which it will be used and to ensure the building blends with the surrounding environment.

"At one level my goal is simply to give people pleasure in being in a space and walking around it. But ... architecture can reach a level where it influences people to want to do something more with their lives. That is the challenge that I find most interesting."

Inspired by gardens and buildings

Ieoh Ming Pei was born on April 26, 1917, in Canton (now Guangzhou), China. He was the second of five children. His father, Tsuyee Pei, came from a wealthy family and worked as an executive with the Bank of China. Pei's mother, Lien Kwun, was a musician. She was devoutly religious and took her son to Buddhist temples in mountain sanctuaries. These trips and the gardens at the Pei family refuge in

I. M. Pei. *AP/World Wide Photos.*

What's in a Name?

Pei's name, Ieoh Ming, means "to inscribe brightly"—an appropriately descriptive name for someone who went on to design buildings that were appreciated as works of art.

Suzhou, called "Garden of the Lion Forest," inspired his love of nature.

Pei had a happy childhood, but it was not without disruptions. Because of unrest among warlords, or regional leaders who ruled by force, his family relocated from inland China to the port city of Hong Kong, which was then a British colony, when he was an infant. Pei learned English in Hong Kong, which came in handy when his family moved to Shanghai, China, when he was ten. He enrolled in a school run by English Protestant missionaries. The school was difficult: Students were allowed only a half day a month away from school for recreation. At the age of thirteen, Pei's mother died.

Pei's father hoped his son would study medicine and become a doctor. However, Pei was inspired by modern buildings being erected in Shanghai and decided to study architecture in the United States. In 1935, at the age of seventeen, he boarded the SS *Coolidge* for an ocean voyage to America.

School and marriage in Boston

Pei began his architectural studies at the University of Pennsylvania but stayed there for only two weeks. The architectural program emphasized drawing, and he was interested in engineering and practical approaches to construction. He transferred to the Massachusetts Institute of Technology in Cambridge, just outside of Boston, where he was able to combine architecture and engineering. Upon graduating in 1940, Pei planned to return home, but World War II (1939–45) was underway and China was invaded by Japan.

Pei found architectural work in Boston, and he also traveled to New York City and Los Angeles, California, on projects. In Boston, he met Eileen Loo, a Chinese American who had recently graduated from college. They were married in 1942 and would have four children, Ting, Chien, Li, and Liane.

Pei's wife enrolled in the landscape architecture program at the Harvard Graduate School of Design. Pei won a fellowship, or a special scholarship, to the same school to pursue a master's degree in architecture. The United States was involved in World War II, and in January 1943, Pei left school to work for the National Defense Research Committee in Princeton, New Jersey. Pei was involved in experimental projects in which buildings were destroyed.

Pei returned to Harvard in 1944 and earned his master's degree in architecture in 1946. He was an assistant professor at Harvard for a short time and again considered returning to China. China was embroiled in a civil war, however, and it was dangerous for the Peis to travel there.

In 1948, Pei joined Webb and Knapp, a New York City firm that developed construction projects, as director of architecture. Among other projects, Pei designed a roof garden and dining room for the company headquarters that offered a spectacular view of the New York City skyline. Pei launched his own New York City architectural firm, I. M. Pei & Associates, in 1955.

During the 1950s, Pei was involved in large-scale development projects in Chicago, Denver, and New York City. Through this experience of designing new buildings to be constructed near older structures, Pei developed his sensitivity as to how buildings would relate to the surrounding environment.

The first project to bring widespread recognition to Pei's firm was his design for the National Center for Atmospheric Research in Boulder, Colorado. Set in the Rocky Mountains, this was the first project Pei worked on that was not surrounded by other structures. Pei designed the building to blend visually with the surrounding mountain peaks. That project began in 1961 and was competed in 1967.

Prestigious library and museum commissions

Pei's growing reputation earned him a prestigious assignment in 1964. A year after the assassination of President John F. Kennedy (1917–1963; served 1961–63), Kennedy's widow, Jacqueline (1929–1994), selected Pei to design the John F. Kennedy Memorial Library Complex in Boston. The project went through three different design phases, the site was changed three times, and fifteen years passed before the complex was completed in 1979, but it was well worth the effort and patience Pei exerted. The Library was roundly praised

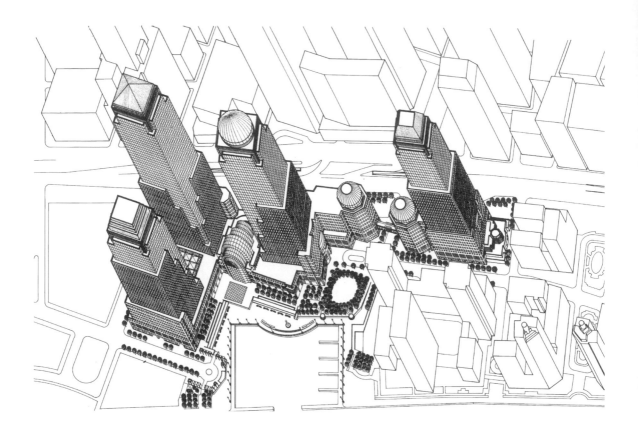

An illustration of the National Gallery of Art, including the East Building structure designed by I. M. Pei. *Botond Bognar.*

when completed and earned Pei a gold medal from the American Institute of Architects.

During this period, Pei won another major commission, this one from the National Gallery of Art in Washington, D.C. Pei was to design a new structure (the East Building) to complement the existing National Gallery of Art (now called the West Building). The project was complicated: the available site was an unusual trapezoidal piece of land among a crowd of dignified buildings that formed the National Mall, and nearby was Capitol Hill, where the U.S. Congress meets. (A trapezoid is a four-sided figure in which only two of the sides are parallel.)

Pei began his design by sketching a diagonal line across a trapezoid to produce two triangles. In the final design, one triangle formed an exhibition hall, and the other housed offices, a library, and a research center. The buildings are connected through a sky-lit central court with several bridges at various floor levels. The repeated triangle pattern

Some of Pei's Notable Projects

1952–56: Mile High Center, Denver, Colorado
1957–62: Kips Bay Plaza, New York City
1961–66: University Plaza, New York University, New York City
1961–67: National Center for Atmospheric Research, Boulder, Colorado
1964–79: John Fitzgerald Kennedy Library, Boston, Massachusetts
1966–69: Bedford-Stuyvesant Superblock, Brooklyn, New York
1966–71: Cleo Rogers Memorial Library, Columbus, Ohio
1966–77: Municipal Center, Dallas, Texas
1968: Everson Museum of Art, Syracuse, New York
1968–73: Herbert F. Johnson Museum of Art, Cornell University, Ithaca, New York
1968–78: National Gallery of Art, Washington, D.C. (east wing)
1970: Wilmington Tower, Wilmington, Delaware
1970–76: Overseas-Chinese Banking Corporation Headquarters, Singapore, China
1977–81: Museum of Fine Arts, Boston, Massachusetts (west wing)
1978–82: Texas Commerce Tower/United Energy Plaza, Houston, Texas
1979–82: Fragrant Hill Hotel, Beijing, China
1982–89: Meyerson Symphony Center, Dallas, Texas
1982–89: Bank of China, Hong Kong
1983–89: Le Grand Louvre (including the Pyramide), Paris, France (expansion: Phase I)
1988–90: Sinji Shumeikai Bell Tower, Shiga, Japan
1991–95: Rock and Roll Hall of Fame, Cleveland, Ohio
1999–2003: German Historical Museum, Berlin, Germany

appears throughout the design, from pieces of marble laid in the floor to steel frames that hold skylights. The National Gallery project, which took ten years to complete (1968 to 1978), made Pei one of the best-known architects in America. Pei succeeded in adding a visually striking new building that blended with the impressive structures surrounding it.

International recognition

Pei's reputation spread overseas. He was commissioned to design a bank building in Singapore in 1976. During the 1980s, he returned to China for the first time since he left in

1935 to design the Fragrant Hill Hotel near Beijing. Completed in 1983, the hotel blends modern forms and traditional Chinese architecture. For inspiration, Pei drew on his childhood memories of the Garden of the Lion Forest. That led him to include a courtyard, gardens of various sizes, and lotus-shaped windows in the hotel. Pei wanted to contribute more to growth and improvement in his native land. When he received the prestigious Prizker Architecture Prize in 1983, he used the $100,000 award to establish a scholarship fund for Chinese men and women to study architecture in the United States.

Pei was soon involved in another deeply personal project in Asia. He was commissioned to design the Bank of China Tower in Hong Kong, which was completed in 1989. The bank had first opened a branch office in Hong Kong in the 1920s—and Pei's father was the first bank manager there. Because Hong Kong is small and land is costly, Pei had to design a skyscraper, but the building had to be able to withstand typhoon winds. In a 1996 interview with *Technology Review* magazine, Pei described how he arrived at the solution for this challenge: "I thought about the triangle, which is the strongest structural form. If the building could essentially consist of shafts with triangular cross sections, it would automatically be very, very rigid. So I made some three-sided sticks and played with them at home, combining them in various arrangements."

Pei began what he called "the greatest challenge and the greatest accomplishment of my career" in 1983 when he was commissioned to expand the most famous art museum in the world—the Louvre, in Paris, France. Before accepting the job, he conducted four months of secret research. He visited the Louvre several times to evaluate what needed to be done to better accommodate the millions of people who toured the museum each year. He wanted to preserve and respect the classic, seventeenth-century design, but also take advantage of advances in modern architecture.

Pei's solution was both classical and modern—a large pyramid made of glass. Visitors pass through the pyramid and descend to an underground entrance lobby. They can then enter each wing of the museum through a series of corridors. The visual beauty of the original building was not only preserved, but visitors were now also able to view it through the glass of the pyramid—as a work of art might be seen in a mu-

seum. A main pyramid was constructed with 698 panes of glass, and three
satellite pyramids stand nearby.

Rockin' in his seventies

Pei designed dozens of other
structures during his career. Among
the most intriguing was his commission for the Rock and Roll Hall of
Fame, which opened in 1995 and was
significant to the revitalization of
downtown Cleveland, Ohio. A jazz
fan all his life, Pei realized that he
needed to familiarize himself with the
music in order to capture the spirit of
rock and roll in his design. "The prob-
lem was that I didn't like the music," Pei told *Technology Review.* "My children loved it, but I never did. And yet, since I
was selected to do the project, I had to learn about the music.
So I went to Graceland to see Elvis Presley's home. I went to
Louisiana to listen to jazz and rhythm and blues. And then I
began to understand the rich roots of rock and roll."

The spirit Pei determined to capture was a sense of rebellion, of breaking away from tradition, with a dimension of
energy. He designed a six-story central tower and an adjacent,
117-foot-high triangular glass wall. "The generation that made
rock music was much more transparent [straightforward] about
their ideas than my generation," Pei told Michael J. Crosbic in
an interview with *Progressive Architecture* magazine. Pei symbolized that transparency though the wall of glass. "These are the
things I tried to imbue [build into] in the building's design—a
sense of tremendous youthful energy, rebellion, flailing
about," Pei explained to *Technology Review* magazine in 1995.
"Part of the museum is a glass tent leaning on a column in the
back. All the other forms—wings—burst out of that tent. Their
thrusting out has to do with rebellion. This, for me, is an expression of the musical form of rock and roll." The museum
also features state-of-the-art lighting and multimedia displays.

In 1990, Pei retired from the firm he had founded and
began to work independently. Along with the Rock and Roll
Hall of Fame, Pei's projects in the 1990s included the private

 Pei on Critics

"I welcome critics because they
are bound to have good reasons for their
concerns," Pei told *Technology Review*
magazine in a 1995 interview. "But rather
than generalizing about my work, they
should look at each project by itself. The
basic challenges in building design differ
from project to project, and critics have to
understand those—where a project is
built, and why."

Miho Museum in Japan, which opened in 1997. Located in the Shigaraki Mountains on a nature preserve, the museum was named after Mihoko Koyama, the spiritual leader of the Shinji Shumeikai religious group. In some ways, this project allowed Pei to come full circle in his life, to connect his early love of nature he discovered in Buddhist sanctuaries and his family's Garden of the Lion Forest with an artistic view of structures that inspired him to become an architect. Not surprisingly, when he is not designing buildings, Pei enjoys gardening around his home in Katonah, New York.

—*Roger Matuz*

For More Information

Books

Pei, I. M., and Von Boehm, Gero. *Conversations with I. M. Pei: Light Is the Key.* New York: Prestel, 2000.

Wiseman, Carter. *I. M. Pei, A Profile in American Architecture.* Rev. ed. New York: Harry N. Abrams, 2001.

Periodicals

Crosbie, Michael J. "Raising Rock's Reliquary." *Progressive Architecture* (February 1995): pp. 62–65.

"I. M. Pei: A Feeling for Technology and Art." *Technology Review* (April 1995): pp. 59–62.

Web Sites

"Architect: I. M. Pei." *Great Buildings.* http://www.greatbuildings.com/architects/I._M._Pei.html (accessed on March 23, 2004).

"I. M. Pei." *Pei Cobb Freed & Partners.* http://www.pcfandp.com/a/f/fme/imp/b/b.html (accessed on March 23, 2004).

Joseph Priestley

Born March 24, 1733
Fieldhead, England

Died February 6, 1804
Northumberland, Pennsylvania

Scientist, philosopher, teacher, minister

Joseph Priestley is credited for being one of the founding fathers of the science known as chemistry. In addition to discovering oxygen, he conducted experiments with fixed air (carbon dioxide), which eventually led to the development of carbonated beverages, or soda pop. His good friend Benjamin Franklin (1706–1790) aroused his interest in electricity, and it was Priestley who discovered that graphite is a useful electrical conductor. In addition to his scientific interests, Priestley was a published philosopher whose beliefs differed from the religious majority of the day. As a result, he and his family were outcasts, subjected to ridicule and physical violence. Priestley brought to America a new religion—Unitarianism—although the movement would not be referred to as such for years to come.

"Truth can never have a fair chance of being discovered, or propagated, without the most perfect freedom of inquiry and debate."

A curious mind leads to internal conflict

Joseph Priestley was born the oldest of six siblings to Jonas (a weaver) and Mary (a farmer's daughter) near Leeds, England, on March 13, 1733. When the Gregorian calendar

Joseph Priestley.
International Portrait Gallery.

(the one used today) came into use in 1751, Priestley changed his birth date to March 24. Because the six children were born close together, Mary sent her eldest child to live with her parents while he was young. He returned to the Priestley home upon his mother's death, only to be adopted by his father's sister at the age of nine. During his stay with his aunt, Priestley was introduced to philosophical and religious discussions as well as liberal (open to new ideas) political attitudes. He lived with his aunt Sarah until her death in 1764.

Although Priestly attended local schools throughout his childhood, he was stricken with tuberculosis, an infectious disease of the lungs, while still a teenager and was forced to drop out. His illness did not prevent him from learning, however. He used the time to teach himself French, German, Italian, and several other languages. In addition, he also learned the basics of geometry, algebra, and mathematics.

After recovering from his bout with tuberculosis, the young Priestley was determined to begin training for the career goal he had always envisioned, that of the ministry. After living in a household in which lively discussion of religion and politics was an everyday occurrence, however, he found himself questioning some of the basic beliefs of the Calvinist faith, a religion that embraces a particularly stern and rigid moral code. In particular, Priestley did not believe in the trinity—the Father, Son, and Holy Ghost. Rather than attend the strict religious academy near his home, he chose to attend the more liberal Daventry Academy. There he had the chance to learn not just traditional subjects, but those involving natural and experimental philosophy as well. While at the academy, his inclination for and interest in experimentation was nurtured.

Interest in science, priority in theology

Although he clearly possessed scientific interests and abilities, Priestley remained intent on becoming a minister. Upon graduation from Daventry, he accepted a position with a poverty-stricken congregation in Suffolk. However, he was not successful, largely due to his Unitarian tendencies. The Unitarian faith rejects the concept of the trinity, and though it upholds the moral teachings of Jesus, it denies his status as divine, believing instead that God exists as only one being.

Priestley eagerly accepted an invitation to preach in Cheshire, where churchgoers were more apt to accept his theology. In addition to preaching, Priestley became schoolmaster and private tutor, a promotion that brought with it an increase in salary. He used the extra income to fund his private research.

He grew in popularity at Cheshire and eventually accepted a position as tutor at a Dissenting Academy in Warrington. Dissenting Academies were the center of liberal education in this era as traditional universities did not welcome dissenters, or people whose beliefs were not in keeping with the conformist beliefs and theories of the time. Priestley spent six years at Warrington. In 1762, he married Mary Wilkinson, daughter of English inventor John Wilkinson (1728–1808).

Career takes a turn

While still at Warrington, Priestley applied for an ordination to the Dissenting ministry a month before his wedding was to take place. His application was accepted, and he began giving lectures on history and general policy in the hopes of opening previously unexplored academic roads to his students. He became a popular public speaker.

Priestly enjoyed an annual month-long trip to London, during which time he met with other distinguished dissenters. While on one of these visits, he became friends with Benjamin Franklin. Their friendship encouraged Priestley's natural interests in experimentation, and he soon discovered the use of graphite as an electrical conductor. Through the American statesman, Priestley was introduced to the scientific community at large, and his first scientific paper, *The History and Present State of Electricity,* was published. The paper included results from his original experiments. As a result of his publication, he was elected as a Fellow of the Royal Society in 1766. When it became clear that the paper was too difficult for the ordinary reader to understand, Priestley set out to publish another edition, this time with illustrations. When he was unable to find anyone to make the drawings, he did them himself. During the course of his work, he accidentally discovered the use of India rubber as an eraser of pencil markings. Thus, the crude version of the modern pencil eraser was born.

An engraved drawing of Joseph Priestley. *Library of Congress.*

Not long after his debut into the publishing world, Priestley became the minister at Mill Hill. He moved his family to Mill Chapel in Leeds in 1767. His most important discoveries began that year, as his focus changed from that of electricity to air. Priestley had convenient access to fixed air (carbon dioxide), as his house was situated near a brewery. Through repeated experimentation, the scientist eventually discovered that bubbles, or effervescence, found in sparkling beverages and natural spas were really the result of nothing more than water that contained fixed air. The paper he wrote and published on this subject won him the impressive Copley Medal of the Royal Society.

Discovers oxygen

Although Priestley is credited with discovering oxygen, it is more correct to say that he isolated dephlogisticated air, the term once used for oxygen. In 1774, Priestley was working with another scientist, Carl Scheele (1742–1786). Scheele figured out that heating liquids results in the release of gas, and using this information, Priestley isolated oxygen by heating mercuric oxide. Upon making his discovery, he is quoted as saying, "I have discovered an air five or six times as good as common air." One hundred years after the scientist's greatest contribution to chemistry, he was honored for his discovery at a meeting that led to the founding of the American Chemical Society.

Priestley left Leeds to accept a position as librarian and tutor for William Petty (1737–1805), Earl of Shelburne. He received a generous salary, and it was during this time that he published the works for which he is most famous: *Disqui-*

sitions Relating to Matter and Spirit and *Experiments and Observations.* After enjoying a productive period as a chemist from 1773 to 1780, Priestley quit his job with Lord Shelburne on good terms and left to resume a life in the ministry.

Immigrates to America amid controversy

By this time, Priestley's family had grown to include three sons and a daughter. He moved them to Birmingham, England, in 1780 and joined the Lunar Society, a group of about a dozen men with similar interests. Commonly referred to as "Lunatics," these men were interested in natural science and literature as well as all things metaphysical (involving the supernatural, among other things). They met once a month on the Monday nearest the full moon. This particular time was chosen so that the members could travel home by moonlight, able to see but not necessarily seen by others who might not agree with what the Lunatics had been doing.

During these years in Birmingham, Priestley wrote a number of philosophical and religious works. The publication of these writings caused great controversy. Their author, whose beliefs got him labeled a dissenter, was attacked in magazines and pamphlets as well as in churches. He was considered an agent of the Devil.

In eighteenth–century England, dissenters were deprived the rights of citizenship and those considered Unitarian could not legally be tolerated. With the commencement of the French Revolution (1789–99), dissenters sided with those citizens who were being oppressed by the government. In July 1791, a dinner was to be held to celebrate Bastille Day, a celebration of independence in France, similar to the Fourth of July in America. Priestley disappointed the crowds raging outside the hotel where the dinner was held by not attending. Later in the evening, the rioters regrouped, and, under the influence of alcohol, burned down the New Meetinghouse where Priestley preached. They also burned down the Old Meetinghouse. Someone ran ahead and warned Priestley of the approaching mob, and Priestley and his wife left their home with only the clothes they were wearing. They stopped at a neighbor's home, only to realize the rioters were already at their home, looking for them. As they moved on, they looked back in time to see their home ablaze. Priestley lost all his earthly possessions, including his unpublished papers and his science lab.

The Priestleys escaped to London but found little peace. Priestley continued to be attacked from church pulpits and in pamphlets, and now he was receiving letters threatening his life. An honorary citizen of France as a result of his support during the Revolution, he was denounced, or criticized, by the Royal Society and forced to resign his membership. It was clear that neither he nor his family were welcome in London, so they immigrated to America, leaving London on April 7, 1794. Priestley had just turned sixty-one.

America welcomes the persecuted

Once in America, Priestley took his family to Philadelphia, Pennsylvania, where he joined one of his sons and a mutual friend, Thomas Cooper, in hopes of establishing a colony for English Dissenters. The colony never became reality, and the family moved to Northumberland, a small town on the banks of the Susquehanna River. Tragedy struck within the year, however, when both Priestley's wife and youngest son died. Although Priestley kept himself busy with experiments and preaching, he was no longer the cheerful man he once was.

Lonely for intellectual discussion and company, Priestley spent the long winter months in Philadelphia. He founded the first Unitarian Church there, and his sermons were highly regarded by some of the most prestigious thinkers of the day, including future presidents John Adams (1735–1826; served 1797–1801) and Thomas Jefferson (1743–1826; served 1801–9). Jefferson admired Priestley and consulted with him on important matters, such as the content of the curriculum of the University of Virginia, which he was planning to establish. Clearly, Priestley had found a home where his differing views were considered cause for celebration rather than condemnation.

In 1801, the aging Priestley fell ill, and he never fully recovered his health. On February 5, 1804, he had his children brought to his bedside, where he encouraged them to continue in their love for one another. He died quietly the following day at the age of seventy-one and was buried next to his beloved wife and son.

—Rebecca Valentine

For More Information

Books

Hirsch, Alison Duncan, and Kyle R. Weaver. *Joseph Priestley House: Pennsylvania Trail of History Guide*. Mechanicsburg, PA: Stackpole Books, 2003.

Horvitz, Leslie Alan. *Eureka! Scientific Breakthroughs That Changed the World*. Hoboken, NJ: Wiley, 2001.

Schofield, Robert E. *The Enlightenment of Joseph Priestley: A Study of His Life and Work from 1733 to 1773*. University Park: Pennsylvania State University Press, 1997.

Web Sites

Silverman, Sharon Hernes. "Joseph Priestley, Catalyst of the Enlightenment." Originally printed in *Pennsylvania Heritage Magazine*. Available on *Pennsylvania Historical and Museum Commission* Web site. http://www.phmc.state.pa.us/ppet/priestley/page1.asp?secid=31 (accessed on March 23, 2004).

Stelter, Eric, and Susana Suarez. "Joseph Priestley." *The History of Chemistry: 1992 Woodrow Wilson Summer Institute*. http://www.woodrow.org/teachers/chemistry/institutes/1992/Priestley.html (accessed on March 23, 2004).

Joseph Pulitzer

Born April 10, 1847
Mako, Hungary

Died October 29, 1911
Charleston, South Carolina

Publisher who created mass-circulation newspapers that strongly affected government policy

"Our Republic and its press will rise or fall together. An able, disinterested, public-spirited press, with trained intelligence to know the right and courage to do it, can preserve that public virtue without which popular government is a sham and a mockery."

Joseph Pulitzer. *Getty Images.*

Joseph Pulitzer is considered the inventor of the modern newspaper as a part of the mass media, which today refers to an entertainment or information source, including print and electronic sources, designed to appeal to a very large audience rather than to a narrower audience of people with special interests. He turned newspapers, which had been largely devoted to political parties and causes, into an entertainment medium. By doing so, Pulitzer achieved political influence for newspapers that had not existed before.

Young man overcomes early odds

Joseph Pulitzer was born in Mako, Hungary, the son of a well-to-do grain merchant. Pulitzer's father Philip was from a Hungarian-German Jewish family; his mother, Louise, was a Roman Catholic. When Joseph Pulitzer was six, his father had made enough money to retire to Budapest, Hungary's capital, where he paid for private tutors to educate his children. Pulitzer grew up speaking three languages fluently: Hungarian, German, and French.

Pulitzer was never healthy, not even as a young boy. He was thin, his lungs were weak, and his vision was poor. Poor health would plague Pulitzer throughout his life.

By age seventeen, Pulitzer was restless, ambitious, and eager for adventure. He tried to enlist in the Austrian Army, but he was turned down because of his poor eyesight. He was rejected in turn by the French Foreign Legion and the British Army. Finally, while traveling in Germany, Pulitzer met an agent for the U.S. Army looking for soldiers to fight in the American Civil War (1861–65). During the Civil War, American young men were subjected to being drafted, or ordered to report for service, but they could avoid serving by paying a fee of $300. This money was then used to attract other men to fight in the Army. American recruiters often looked for candidates in Germany.

Pulitzer enlists, moves to America

Accepted as a soldier at last, Pulitzer sailed for the United States, where he had a plan to collect money for enlisting in the Army to fight for the North in the Civil War. When his ship was near Boston, Massachusetts, on its way to New York, Pulitzer jumped overboard and swam to shore. His plan was to enlist and collect the enlistment bonus instead of sharing it with the agent who recruited him in Germany.

The year was 1864. On September 30, Pulitzer enlisted in a cavalry regiment, or horse-mounted troops, being organized by Carl Schurz (1829–1906), a prominent German American who would be highly influential later in Pulitzer's life. Pulitzer's military career did not last long. He was a soldier in the Union cavalry for less than a year. The Civil War ended just six months after he joined the Army, and Pulitzer was discharged from the Army in July 1865.

What was a tall, bearded young man to do, especially one who did not speak English well and had little money? Pulitzer decided to head for St. Louis, Missouri, where there was a large colony of German-speaking immigrants, including his regiment leader, Schurz.

In St. Louis, Pulitzer did what many other young immigrants did: he found a series of odd jobs to feed himself and pay rent. Pulitzer tended mules, waited on tables in a restau-

Pulitzer, Schurz, and Liberal Republicans

Joseph Pulitzer got his start in journalism when the commander of his Civil War army unit, Carl Schurz, offered him a job on the *Westliche Post,* a German-language paper of which Schurz was editor and part owner. Schurz himself was an immigrant from Germany who was active in the Republican Party.

In the middle of the nineteenth century, journalism and politics were closely linked. Schurz had edited several papers in Midwestern cities before coming to St. Louis, and he was regarded as a spokesman for the country's large and influential German American community. Schurz had always been an advocate of honest government and was a stern critic of the policies of President Ulysses S. Grant (1822–1885; served 1869–77) following the Civil War.

Schurz was elected to the U.S. Senate from Missouri in 1869 and was active in

Carl Schurz, Joseph Pulitzer's cavalry leader and fellow German American, who later introduced Pulitzer to publishing. *Library of Congress.*

the unsuccessful 1872 presidential campaign of Horace Greeley (1811–1872) as a Liberal Republican and Democrat. (Greeley lost to President Grant and, in fact, died less than a month after the election.)

rant, and drove a horse-drawn taxi. As a well-educated young man who had grown up in comfortable circumstances, Pulitzer did not settle for unskilled jobs for long. He worked for several lawyers, which was the way people studied the law in the nineteenth century, and within two years he had learned enough about the law to be admitted to the bar, which qualified him to practice law. But the law was not to be his future.

In St. Louis, his acquaintance from the war, Schurz, was editor and part-owner of a German-language newspaper called the *Westliche Post,* which was influential among the city's large German population. Schurz offered Pulitzer a position as a reporter on his newspaper. Pulitzer threw himself into his new job, following Schurz's lead in uncovering government corruption in which city officials accepted bribes, or payoffs, from companies doing business with the city. Pulitzer quickly gained a reputation in the city, and in 1869 he was nominated to run for the state legislature as a Republican. Although his district usually voted for Democrats, Pulitzer was elected and served in the legislature while still writing for the *Westliche Post.*

Pulitzer becomes a newspaper publisher

In 1872, Pulitzer made what may have been the single biggest move in his life: He bought the struggling *St. Louis Post* for about $3,000 (worth about $40,000 in the twenty-first century). The same year, he acquired the *Westliche Post,* which he soon sold at a profit. Pulitzer had left the world of German-language journalism and become owner and editor of a small English-language paper in St. Louis.

The new newspaper publisher threw himself into his job. Already involved in the Liberal Republican crusade against government corruption, Pulitzer used his newspaper to advance the social causes in which he believed. Working with editor John Cockerill (1845–1896), Pulitzer enthusiastically uncovered wrongdoing by city officials, campaigned for street repairs, and fought against gambling and a public lottery. In the nineteenth century, most newspapers were closely linked to a political party; Pulitzer changed this tradition with his paper when he declared it would be an independent, reliable "organ of truth," as Pulitzer wrote in an editorial. Although Pulitzer continued to be associated with the Liberal Republicans, his newspaper became part of the community, read by people of many different parties. Six years after acquiring the *Post,* Pulitzer bought another paper in St. Louis, the *Dispatch,* and combined it with the *Post* to form the *St. Louis Post-Dispatch,* which is still the leading paper in St. Louis a century and a half later.

In the same year that he bought the *Dispatch,* Pulitzer married Kate Davis, who was well connected in St. Louis society. As owner of a successful and leading newspaper in the city, Pulitzer and his wife were almost members of the city's high

High Drama in the Newsroom

Editing a newspaper in the nineteenth century was not always a calm job. On October 13, 1882, an attorney, Civil War veteran, and former candidate for U.S. Congress named Alonzo W. Slayback (1838–1882) burst into the editorial offices of the *St. Louis Post-Dispatch* and confronted editor John Cockerill (1845–1896). His friends claimed that Slayback, accompanied by another attorney, planned to demand an apology for a story in the paper, and perhaps to slap the editor in the face for good measure.

Cockerill, who had a running feud with Slayback, became alarmed and picked up a revolver from his desk. He shot Slayback once, in the heart, killing him. Cockerill insisted he had acted in self-defense and was never charged with murder.

society. Some people in the city never let Pulitzer forget that his father had been Jewish (he had been called "Joey the Jew" when he first arrived). There was something about this upstart immigrant from Hungary that did not quite fit with the fancy clothes and top hats that gentlemen in St. Louis wore in the 1870s and 1880s. The couple eventually had seven children, but by most accounts theirs was not a happy marriage. Within a decade, Pulitzer's health began to fail and he began suffering a series of emotional problems that made him difficult to live with as a husband or as a father.

Pulitzer in New York

In 1882, a shooting involving his editor Joseph Cockerill (see box) added to other strains on Pulitzer's health. The publisher's doctor advised him to take a long, restful vacation in Europe. On his way, however, Pulitzer stopped in New York, where he received an offer to buy the *New York World.* Although he had made a success of the *St. Louis Post-Dispatch,* owning a newspaper in the nation's biggest city and cultural capital was in a different league altogether. The *World* was failing and its owner, businessman Jay Gould (1836–1892), wanted to sell. Pulitzer could not resist the challenge.

Pulitzer immediately threw himself into improving the fortunes of his new newspaper, which had a circulation of about fifteen thousand copies a day. In an effort to compete with the crowded field of daily newspapers in New York, in the era before radio or television, Pulitzer introduced innovations, or new ideas, that would change the face of the entire newspaper industry. In addition to the usual mixture of politics and scandal, Pulitzer added stories about sports to appeal to people interested in that topic. The *World* also helped draw its readers into the world of crime by printing diagrams of crime scenes and publishing details of murder. He even sought to interest young children with the introduction of color cartoons.

Pulitzer experimented with the appearance of his paper. Previously, newspapers looked like a solid mass of gray type. Pulitzer introduced BIG, BOLD HEADLINES that grabbed the readers' attention. His coverage of crime stories later came to be called sensationalism: Screaming headlines about crimes that may have been routine in New York, but which Pulitzer's headlines made seem dramatic and sensational—meant to arouse the senses.

As publisher of the *World,* Pulitzer was in direct competition for readers with another publisher who had started in the West, William Randolph Hearst (1863–1951) of San Francisco, who bought the *New York Morning Journal* in 1895 and launched an evening edition of the paper the following year. Hearst imitated many of Pulitzer's innovations, and the two were fierce competitors, each straining to outdo the other in presenting sensational stories and giant headlines designed to make readers pick one paper over the other on newsstands on the way home from work in the evening. The 1890s were an era when most newspapers were bought from newsstands, rather than being delivered to the home, and when reading the paper was the evening's entertainment.

At the same time, Pulitzer did not lose sight of his earlier focus on government reform. He continued his earlier community crusading with stories about municipal corruption and the need for political reform.

The competition between Pulitzer and Hearst reached its peak in February 1898 when a mysterious explosion rocked the U.S. Navy battleship U.S.S. *Maine,* anchored in the harbor of Havana, Cuba. The ship sank, killing 260 sailors. At the time, Cuba was a possession of Spain, which was putting down a revolt. Pulitzer and Hearst had already been competing to report alleged atrocities, or claims of acts of violence, by the Spanish against the Cuban rebels. The sinking of the *Maine* provided an even better headline, and in their eagerness to build circulation, Pulitzer's *New York World* and Hearst's *New York Journal* generated an enormous war cry. Blaming Spain for the explosion (the source of which has never been made clear), Pulitzer and Hearst demanded that the United States strike back. On April 19, 1898, Congress recognized Cuba's independence, which amounted to a declaration of war against Spain. A short conflict, lasting less than six months, resulted in victory for the United States, giving them control over the Philippines (also a Spanish possession) and Puerto Rico, as well as granting Cuban independence.

Health woes continue

In the 1880s, Pulitzer's eyesight, never strong, began to fail, and by the 1890s he was virtually blind. Making matters worse, Pulitzer suffered from a battery of illnesses: asthma, a lung disease that makes it difficult to breathe; diabetes, a disorder affecting the body's ability to absorb sugar that can lead to many complications, such as blindness, unless treated; insomnia, an inability to fall asleep; and a mental condition called manic depression, which results in wide and sudden mood swings. Pulitzer became very sensitive to noise and felt compelled to live in soundproof rooms he built in his mansions in Bar Harbor, Maine, and New York City and aboard his yacht. After 1890, Pulitzer did not set foot in the newsroom of the *New York World,* communicating instead through secretaries and using a secret code to ensure his messages were not intercepted.

The impact of Pulitzer on the American media

In 1902, Pulitzer laid plans to contribute $2 million to Columbia University in New York to pay for a new school to train journalists. Pulitzer also insisted that money be set aside to award journalists for outstanding work—the Pulitzer Prizes that are so eagerly sought by journalists and are regarded as the profession's top award a century after Pulitzer's death.

There is little doubt that Pulitzer was one of the most influential men in America's newspaper industry. The ideas he pioneered in newspapers are still present in the twenty-first century and are often reflected in television shows specializing in crime or "reality." He transformed publications with circulations geared toward readers of a particular group of people into mass-media enterprises that assumed political influence of their own.

—James L. Outman

For More Information

Books

Barnhurst, Kevin G. *The Form of News: A History.* New York: Guilford Press, 2001.

Brian, Denis. *Pulitzer: A Life.* New York: J. Wiley, 2001.

Douglas, George H. *The Golden Age of the Newspaper.* Westport, CT: Greenwood Press, 1999.

Juergens, George. *Joseph Pulitzer and the New York World.* Princeton, NJ: Princeton University Press, 1966.

Swanberg, W. A. *Pulitzer.* New York: Scribner, 1967.

Periodicals

Davidson, David. "What Made the *World* Great?" *American Heritage* (October-November 1982): p. 62.

Neuharth, Allen H. "The State of News Standards Today Compared with Those in the 'Golden Age.'" *Editor and Publisher* (February 26, 1994): p. 54.

Web Sites

Topping, Seymour. "Joseph Pulitzer and the Pulitzer Prizes." *The Pulitzer Prizes.* http://www.pulitzer.org/History/history.html (accessed on March 23, 2004).

Knute Rockne

Born March 4, 1888
Voss, Norway

Died March 31, 1931
Bazaar, Kansas

College football player and coach

"[A football star must have] brains, courage, self-restraint, co-ordination, fire of nervous energy and an unselfish point of view. Of course, he must have a bit of speed and a bit of physique, but then these things are taken for granted."

Knute Rockne. *Library of Congress.*

As a legendary player and coach for the University of Notre Dame, Knute Rockne helped to change the game of football and increase its popularity. A player from 1911 to 1913, he helped lead Notre Dame to three straight undefeated seasons. The 1913 team revolutionized football by using the forward pass more frequently; rushing, or running, the football had been the standard and dominant way football was played since American football was introduced three decades earlier. As a coach from 1918 to 1930, Rockne led his team to five more undefeated seasons, and Notre Dame won nearly 90 percent of its games under his leadership.

Rockne's teams played before overflow crowds throughout the country, and many of the school's players became famous. Coach Rockne was the most famous of all—a colorful speaker and tireless promoter of football as well as an exceptional motivator and football strategist. The nation was shocked when he died in a plane crash at the age of forty-three in 1931. The popular 1940 film *Knute Rockne: All American* recalled his life and his ability to motivate players.

Academic and athletic

Knute Kenneth Rockne was born in Voss, Norway, on March 4, 1888, the second child and only son among five children of Lars Knutson and Martha (Gjermo) Rockne. His father was an engineer who traveled to the United States in 1891 to work on a carriage he invented and wanted to exhibit at the Columbian Exposition in Chicago, Illinois, a fair that showed new inventions from around the world. In 1893, the remaining family members joined him, and the Rocknes settled in Chicago.

As a boy, Rockne loved playing and watching sports, especially football and track. He was an excellent student in math and history but soon before graduating from high school his love of sports interfered and cost him a diploma. He cut classes to practice for a track meet. Rockne was suspended and told to transfer to another school, but he never completed his high school education.

Beginning that summer, Rockne held a series of odd jobs: he washed windows, worked on a ferry boat, and picked crops. He passed a Civil Service examination and then worked for four years in the Chicago Post Office. He continued to read and write during this period, saved his money, and won acceptance to the University of Notre Dame in 1910, starting college at the age of twenty-two. Four years later, he graduated with distinction, earning a bachelor of science degree with a specialty in chemistry. He was editor of the annual collection of student writings in his senior year.

Football star

During his college years, Rockne starred as an end on the Notre Dame football team. At 5 feet 8 inches tall and 165 pounds, he was small and fast, which the team used to good advantage. During Rockne's three seasons as a player, Notre Dame did not lose—winning twenty games and playing to two ties. The Fighting Irish of Notre Dame outscored its opponents 879-77 during the period. College football games were played during the months of October and November back then, were dominated by rushing plays (running with the football), and featured teams battling head-to-head, yard by yard. Notre Dame's speed and deceptive plays made it dif-

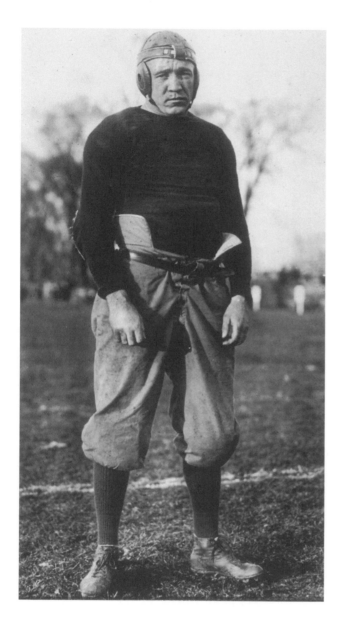

Knute Rockne, as a football player for the University of Notre Dame. *Getty Images.*

ficult to defend. After having been tied twice in 1911, Notre Dame's record was perfect in 1912 (seven wins, no losses, no ties), and it was halfway to another perfect season in 1913. Standing in its way was Army, another football powerhouse.

Notre Dame had a new coach in 1913. His name was Jesse Harper (1884–1961), and unlike his predecessor, John L. Marks, who was successful with the traditional style of football, Harper liked to experiment. He encouraged Rockne, who was the team's captain in 1913, to practice running patterns and having his roommate, quarterback Gus Dorais (1891–1954), throw to him while he was running. During the summer of 1913, they practiced while hanging out at a beach on Lake Michigan. "I'd run along the beach," explained Rockne, "Dorais would throw from all angles. People who didn't know (that) we were two college seniors making painstaking preparations for our final season probably thought we were crazy."

Early in the game against Army, which was playing out as a typical bruising football game, Rockne faked a limp as he went to his end position. When the next play started, Rockne began running downfield, past Army defenders, and Dorais tossed the football to him in full stride, resulting in a long touchdown and six points. "Everybody seemed astonished," said Rockne, afterward. "There had been no hurdling, no tackling, no plunging, no crushing.... Just a long distance touchdown by rapid transit."

Caught off guard by Notre Dame's ability to pass the football, Army changed its strategy and began defending against the pass. Notre Dame ran the football, instead, with great success. When Army changed back to defending against the run, Notre Dame passed. The result was a stunning 35-13 victory for Notre Dame. Football historians agree that Notre Dame's ability to pass the football effectively changed the game of football forever, as the passing game became more important. Notre Dame went on to an undefeated, championship season.

Coaching legend

After he graduated in 1914, Rockne applied to the medical school of Saint Louis University. His admission was denied because of his intention to coach football while studying medicine, which was considered unrealistic by medical school officials. Instead, Rockne was hired by Notre Dame as a chemistry instructor, head track coach, and assistant football coach. He married Bonnie Gwendoline Skiles on July 15, 1914. They would have four children.

Rockne was an assistant football coach under Jesse Harper from the 1914 through 1917 seasons. Notre Dame continued to be successful, but it no longer had the surprise passing game it enjoyed in 1913. Both Army and Yale defeated Notre Dame in 1914. When Harper retired in 1918, Rockne became head football coach. With the United States involved in World War I (1914–18), Notre Dame played only six games that year. In 1919, the war was over and the Rockne coaching legend truly began. The team won all nine games that year, outscoring its opponents 229-47.

Under Rockne's leadership, Notre Dame began developing and showcasing colorful players who had a national following through reports in the press. The first of those players, George Gipp (1895–1920), was convinced to play football by Rockne when he was still an assistant coach. On a campus athletic field one day, he observed Gipp drop-kicking a football up to 70 yards. (The dropkick involves a player taking a few steps for momentum, dropping the ball, and then kicking the ball immediately after it hits the ground. Since footballs were rounder before World War II [1939–45], a player could kick the ball higher and farther by using the dropkick.) Rockne encouraged Gipp, who had come to Notre Dame in 1916 to play baseball and had never played organized foot-

The Gipper

When a mediocre Notre Dame team was trying to salvage a losing season in 1928 by defeating football powerhouse Army, Rockne gave his famous locker-room speech. The team knew of George Gipp's accomplishments, but Rockne told them something they did not know: that on his deathbed, Gipp said to Rockne, "I've got to go, Rock. It's all right, I'm not afraid. Some time, Rock, when the team is up against it, when things are wrong and the breaks are beating the boys, tell them to go in there with all they've got and win just one for the Gipper. I don't know where I'll be then, Rock, but I'll know about it, and I'll be happy." Whether or not Gipp actually said those words is subject to debate. But the deathbed scene and the words spoken by Gipp made for a great scene in a movie.

ball, to try out for the team. By the time Gipp hit the field in a Notre Dame uniform, he could do it all—run, pass, kick, and play on defense. He was named the outstanding college player in America in 1920.

Gipp was fun-loving and broke team rules. In his first college game, for example, Gipp was supposed to punt the ball to the other team, but instead he drop-kicked the ball and turned the play into a sixty-two-yard field goal, a record then and still one of the longest in football history. The three points from the field goal proved to be the margin of victory. Gipp was so popular that Notre Dame's next-to-last game in the 1920 season, his final year of college eligibility, was designated George Gipp Day. But Gipp was ill with fever resulting from a throat infection. He did not play for three quarters on George Gipp Day, and the crowd became increasingly loud, demanding that he play. He entered the game in the fourth quarter and threw two long touchdown passes.

Gipp's days were numbered. His illness turned into pneumonia, and he died on December 14, 1920, less than three weeks after Notre Dame had completed an undefeated season. Rockne would later recall to his 1928 Notre Dame team an exchange he had with his star player while Gipp was on his deathbed. That mediocre 1928 team was trying to salvage a winning season by defeating football powerhouse Army, when Rockne gave his famous locker-room speech. The 4–4 Notre Dame was playing Army in front of more than seventy thousand fans in New York's Yankee Stadium. To motivate his team, Rockne told them about Gipp on his deathbed, and Rockne implored the team to "Win one for the Gipper." The inspired Notre Dame squad went on to defeat Army, 12-6. The deathbed scene and Rockne's speech were recreated in the movie *Knute Rockne: All American*. Gipp was played by a young actor named Ronald Reagan (1911–), who would later become president of the United States. Although Reagan preferred "Dutch" as his nickname, he was fondly called "the Gipper" by his supporters.

National following

Notre Dame posted a 10-1 record in 1921 featuring three stars: Jim Crowley (1902–1986) at left halfback, Don Miller (c. 1902–1972) at right halfback, and Harry Stuhldreher (1901–1965) at quarterback. In 1922, Rockne added Elmer Layden (1903–1973) at fullback. Small and quick, the four became one of the greatest backfields in college football history. They played as a unit, carrying out Rockne's increasingly sophisticated strategies for surprising opponents. They were popular and became nationally renowned after being nicknamed "The Four Horsemen" by sportswriter Grantland Rice (1880– 1954). To complement the Four Horsemen, the hardworking linemen in front of them were nicknamed the Seven Mules.

 The Four Horsemen

Notre Dame, located in South Bend, Indiana, became a nationally popular team in part because of colorful players, some of whom inspired sportswriters. After Notre Dame defeated Army on October 18, 1924, Grantland Rice, one of the best known sportswriters of the day, wrote a memorable story about the Four Horsemen of Notre Dame in the *New York Herald Tribune*:

Outlined against a blue-gray October sky, the Four Horsemen rode again. In dramatic lore they are known as Famine, Pestilence, Destruction and Death. These are only aliases. Their real names are: Stuhldreher, Miller, Crowley and Layden. They formed the crest of the South Bend cyclone before which another fighting Army team was swept over the precipice at the Polo Grounds this afternoon as 55,000 spectators peered down upon the bewildering panorama spread out on the green plain below.

Notre Dame not only continued to win, but it drew ever larger crowds. Rockne was the first football coach to play a national schedule. Total attendance for Notre Dame games in 1921 was over one hundred thousand, but by the end of the 1924 season, it had played in front of over three hundred thousand spectators. The 1924 team was undefeated in nine regular season games and outscored its opponents, 258-44. Notre Dame was invited to play in the Rose Bowl game, held on New Year's Day, 1925, against Stanford University, coached by football great Pop Warner (1871–1954). Notre Dame won 27-10. Beginning in 1927, Notre Dame played an annual game at Soldier's Field in Chicago that alone drew over one hundred thousand fans.

In 1928, Notre Dame played in front of more than four hundred thousand fans, despite a mediocre 5-4 record. That was Rockne's worst record as a coach, but he quickly turned things around. Notre Dame went undefeated in each of Rockne's final two seasons. It won all nine games in 1929, and all of them were played away from the Notre Dame campus because a new football stadium was under construction. In 1930, Notre Dame won all ten games, including a 7-6 thriller over Army before over one hundred thousand fans at Soldier's Field.

Dies at forty-three

Rockne was a colorful man—an excellent speaker who spent much of the off-season touring the country. He was popular with the press and with fans, who enjoyed Notre Dame's exciting offensive play and the football heroes on the team. Rockne promoted his team and his sport in new media of the time, including radio and motion pictures. He conducted summer schools for football coaches, went on tour in Europe, and in 1928 he worked briefly as a sales promotion manager with the Studebaker Corporation, a major automobile manufacturer of the era. He published a nonfiction book, *Coaching* (1925), and a novel, *The Four Winners* (1925).

In 1926, he wrote an article for *Popular Mechanics* titled, "How to Be a Football Star." The most important requirements, wrote Rockne, are "brains, courage, self-restraint, co-ordination, fire of nervous energy and an unselfish point of view. Of course, he must have a bit of speed and a bit of physique, but then these things are taken for granted." The key was hard work. "It is so much pleasanter," wrote Rockne, "to go out and play a game than to spend hours working over tackling, running, signals and other drill points. Without the training, however, there can't be much success in the playing."

The nonstop activity eventually took its toll when Rockne suffered a serious breakdown in 1929. He bounced back by coaching a national championship in 1930 and began to tour again. He was on his way to California for a meeting about a motion picture when the airplane he was flying in crashed in southeastern Kansas on March 31, 1931. He was buried at Notre Dame.

Rockne had made a tremendous and lasting impression on football. Notre Dame, which had been a small college with a little over one hundred students, became a football legend. By 1931, ninety of Rockne's former players had become college coaches, and fifty would become head coaches.

—*Roger Matuz*

For More Information

Books

Robinson, Ray. *Rockne of Notre Dame: The Making of a Football Legend.* New York: Oxford Press, 1999.

Rockne, Bonnie Skiles, ed. *The Autobiography of Knute K. Rockne.* Indianapolis, IN: Bobbs-Merrill Company, 1931.

Steele, Michael R. *Knute Rockne: A Portrait of a Notre Dame Legend.* Champaign, IL: Sports Publishing, 1999.

Periodicals

Chowder, Ken. "When Notre Dame Needed Inspiration, Rockne Provided It." *Smithsonian* (November 1993): pp. 164–77.

Seelhorst, Mary. "Knute Rockne." *Popular Mechanics* (November 2003): pp. 46–47.

Web Sites

"Notre Dame Football Memories: Knute Rockne." *Notre Dame. Official Athletic Site.* http://und.ocsn.com/trads/rockne.html (accessed on March 23, 2004).

Official Knute Rockne Web Site. http://www.cmgww.com/football/rockne/index.html (accessed on March 23, 2004).

John Augustus Roebling

Born June 12, 1806
Mühlhausen, Germany

Died July 22, 1869
Brooklyn, New York

Engineer and bridge designer whose most famous work is New York City's Brooklyn Bridge

"As a great work of art and as a successful specimen of advanced bridge engineering, [the Brooklyn Bridge] will forever testify to the energy, enterprise, and wealth of that community...."

John Augustus Roebling.
Getty Images.

Carving a European-style country out of the North American continent in the nineteenth century was a mammoth undertaking. A key element was building transportation routes across the wild, uncharted territory. Bridges were a vital, if often overlooked, element in both water and surface transportation. John Augustus Roebling, an immigrant from Germany, made two major contributions to the developing nation's transportation: He developed steel ropes, or cables, and he developed the nation's first suspension bridges, which could span longer distances than could bridges made with other technologies.

The story of how Roebling came to be America's first major bridge builder is in most respects typical of how the United States attracted bright young people during the nineteenth century with a promise of a better life than they could expect in Europe, and how in turn these immigrants rewarded their adopted country with talent and innovation that made the miracle of rapid development possible.

Starting out from Germany

After England and Ireland, Germany was the largest

contributor of immigrants to the United States in the new country's first century. Unlike the Irish, who came in an enormous group after the failure of the potato crop in the late 1840s, Germans tended to come in a steady stream. Roebling was typical.

Born in Mühlhausen, Germany, in 1806, the youngest son of Christoph Roebling and his wife Friederike Mueller, John Augustus Roebling was educated in public schools and by tutors to prepare him to attend the Royal Polytechnic Institute in Berlin. (Polytechnic schools prepare students for careers in engineering, architecture, and other fields requiring advanced knowledge of mathematics and physics.) Roebling's mother was said to insist that her children receive a good education, even if it meant sacrificing some of her own private needs. At the Polytechnic Institute, Roebling studied architecture, bridge building, and hydraulics (the science of pumps), as well as languages and philosophy. When he graduated in 1826, he took a government job helping to build roads.

Roebling was not happy with his prospects as a civil engineer (an engineer who designs public projects, like roads) in Germany. He was highly interested in bridges, especially suspension bridges, but his government job did not seem to offer a chance for innovation and challenge. On the other hand, the 1820s and 1830s were a time when Germans were beginning to immigrate to the United States in significant numbers. The country had begun its steady expansion westward, made possible by the defeat of Native American tribes defending their traditional territory and way of life. The market in Europe for American agricultural products was growing, creating a demand for new farms in the United States. It was also a period of intense construction of the new nation's infrastructure, the set of public works like roads and canals that make it possible to travel and carry goods to and from markets.

Roebling planned carefully with his brother Karl. They calculated that their best opportunity lay in farming, and in the spring of 1831, the two brothers set out for Philadelphia, Pennsylvania. They had ruled out settling in the South because both opposed slavery, and they realized that substantial numbers of German emigrants were settling in Pennsylvania.

Traveling by sailing ship, the Roebling brothers arrived in Philadelphia on August 6, 1831. They soon left Philadelphia and headed for Pittsburgh. The early 1830s marked the

Bridge-Building Basics

In building a structure across a space, such as a river, a highway, or a mountainous ravine, there are several different sets of problems. The basic issue is to build the roadbed of the bridge (the part that bears the weight of whatever is to use the bridge, such as cars) so that it does not crack and break into two. The second basic issue is building the roadbed long enough to stretch across the river, or body of water, or whatever the bridge is crossing. The distance across a bridge is called the span.

There are three basic types of bridges. The first type is an arch. Usually made of bricks or stones, an arch is extremely strong but can cover only a limited distance. An arch comprises the ends of the bridge, which look like columns, with an arch between them. The arch itself is usually made of bricks, cut so that they form a half-circle. When weight is put on the roadbed, the bricks are, in effect, squeezed together even more tightly, so that the arch supports the span. Arches are usually the shortest bridges.

The second type of bridge is a truss. A truss is, in its essence, a strong beam that goes across the span. In order to prevent having the beam sag in the middle, engineers actually use two beams, an upper and a lower one, in between which are supports arranged as triangles. The triangles keep the top and bottom beam separated and also enable the beams to bear more weight. A

high point of canals in the United States—essentially man-made rivers along which flat-bottomed boats were pulled by horses or mules walking alongside the canal. When the Pennsylvania Canal, spanning the state from east to west, reached the Allegheny Mountains in the center of the state, the canal boats had to be taken out of the water and placed in special wagons that could be pulled along a smooth surface called the Allegheny Portage Railroad. The railroad, which was nothing like modern railroads, was nevertheless a key link in the Pennsylvania canal system. The railroad for the boats demonstrated the principal drawback of canals: they needed to be flat (so that the water in these shallow rivers did not flow out). Canals were poorly suited for mountains or hilly terrain.

Twenty-five miles from Pittsburgh, the two brothers bought a significant plot of land, about 7,000 acres, near a community of other German immigrants. The town was named Germania, but later changed its name to Saxonburg. Other Germans from Mühlhausen, encouraged by letters simpler version of a truss is the I-beam, a long piece of metal with two flat, wide parts on top and bottom and a thin vertical piece in the middle. Looked at from one end, an I-beam looks like a capital I.

The third type of bridge is the suspension bridge. In this case, a long, strong cable is stretched from shore to shore, across the tops of two tall towers, forming a shape like a capital M. The V shape in the middle of the M is formed by the cable, while the vertical strokes on the M are the two towers. Normally, the cables extend beyond the towers and are attached to a large anchor buried into the ground at either end. Vertical bars are hung from the cables and attached to the upper surface of the roadbed. To make the roadbed even stronger, a truss-type bridge is constructed. In a suspension bridge, the roadway basically hangs from the cables.

The advantage of suspension bridges is that the cables between the towers can be quite long. If they are thick enough and strong enough, they can hold up the roadway. A disadvantage is that suspension bridges may sway in a strong wind, putting stress on the structure and possibly causing it to fall.

The importance of the cables was well understood by John Roebling, America's first master suspension-bridge builder, since he pioneered the so-called wire rope.

from the Roebling brothers, also moved to Saxonburg. In 1837, Roebling married Johanna Herting, the daughter of one of those immigrants.

After six years, however, Roebling's farming venture was not proving to be a success, largely because the land he and his brother had purchased was not suited for the purpose. On top of this, Roebling missed engineering, the work he had been trained for and enjoyed.

Wire rope

In 1838, a year after his marriage, Roebling traveled to Harrisburg, the state capital, and applied for a job as an engineer for the state government. He also became an American citizen in the same year. Employed by the state of Pennsylvania, Roebling worked on a variety of projects: designing more canals, building dams on the Beaver River, and surveying a route for a railroad across the Alleghenies.

The Allegheny Portage Railroad provided Roebling with his first major success. The route of the railroad went up and down the steep hills of the Alleghenies. A complex system of thick ropes was used to haul the canal boat carriages up and down the hills. These ropes, which were about 3 inches thick, were made from hemp, a plant whose fibers were especially suited to manufacturing woven ropes. The ropes tended to fray, which meant they had to be replaced often.

Roebling envisioned a new type of rope, made of twisted wire. The so-called wire rope would resist fraying, and could be made of a smaller diameter while providing superior strength. The thinner wire ropes would be easier to handle, as well as lasting longer.

Roebling presented his idea for "wire rope" to the state officials in charge of the Pennsylvania canal and, after a delay, convinced the state to try his idea. Roebling returned to Saxonburg where he designed machinery to manufacture the rope and set up a factory. Ironically, Roebling's invention came just at the end of the era of using canals, as railroads using steam engines and running on iron tracks replaced the artificial waterways. To Roebling, however, it did not make a difference. His wire rope found many other markets where stronger, smaller, and longer-lasting cables were used to replace hemp ropes. After a few years operating his factory in Saxonburg, Roebling moved his operation to Trenton, New Jersey, where it remained a family-owned business for generations.

Back to bridges

While manufacturing wire rope provided a comfortable living for Roebling, it was not his first love. Even while operating his factory, Roebling had been active in designing structures. From 1844 to 1850, Roebling built several aqueducts to carry water along the Pennsylvania Canal. Aqueducts are structures designed to carry water; in the case of the Pennsylvania Canal, the aqueducts were the equivalent of bridges, letting the canal flow over gorges or ravines. Between 1844 and 1850, Roebling designed and directed the building of at least six canal aqueducts.

In 1846, Roebling also designed the Smithfield Street Bridge across the Monongahela River in Pittsburgh. Five years

Brooklyn Bridge painters walk across the structure on a suspension wire in 1926. © *Hulton-Deutsch Collection/Corbis.*

Boats pass underneath the Brooklyn Bridge. *Harvard University Library.*

later, Roebling designed a bridge over the Niagara River in Niagara Falls, New York. Roebling's specialty was suspension bridges, or suspension aqueducts, a form of bridge that can span much greater distances than other forms of bridges (see box).

In 1867, Roebling, joined by his son Washington Roebling (1837–1926), launched their biggest and most famous project: a bridge connecting two parts of New York City, Manhattan Island on the west and Brooklyn on the east. (Brooklyn, once a city entirely separate from Manhattan but now part of New York City, is situated on the western end of Long Island.) The bridge needed to be high enough to allow ships to pass underneath.

Roebling had first proposed building a bridge between Manhattan and Brooklyn in June 1857. It took a decade before the project was approved and Roebling was named chief engineer. It took two more years for final plans to be made and approved. But before construction could actually begin, Roebling's foot was mashed by a ferry boat while he was standing on a pier, making observations on the bridge site. Roebling was taken to his son's home in Brooklyn and several injured toes were amputated. Although serious, the injury was not thought to be life threatening. But a few days later, the wound became infected. In an age before antibiotics, or drugs that kill the microorganisms that cause infection, Roebling died three weeks after the accident, never seeing the world-famous bridge that is associated with his name.

Roebling's son Washington, who had worked as his assistant, took over. The statistics of the Brooklyn Bridge give a flavor for the size of the project. The total length of the bridge is over a mile—5,989 feet; the distance between the towers is 3,460 feet, a record distance when it was built. The roadbed is 85 feet wide. Four huge cables stretch from each shore, over the tops of two towers. Each cable is 15¾ inches in diameter and 3,578 feet long. The towers are each 276 feet above the surface of the river. The towers were anchored in bedrock, the thick rock that lies under the bed of the river. The foundation of the east tower is 44½ feet under the surface of the water; the west tower, near Manhattan, is 78½ feet below the surface of the water. The roadway is 119 feet above the water at high tide, enough for both steamships and sailing vessels to pass beneath. The project took fifteen years to complete; it opened on May 24, 1883.

—*James L. Outman*

For More Information

Books

Kranakis, Eda. *Constructing a Bridge: An Exploration of Engineering Culture, Design, and Research in Nineteenth-Century France and America.* Cambridge, MA: MIT Press, 1997.

McCullough, David G. *The Great Bridge*. New York: Simon & Schuster, 1972. Reprint, 2001.

Schuyler, Hamilton. *The Roeblings: A Century of Engineers, Bridge-Builders, and Industrialists*. Princeton, NJ: Princeton University Press, 1931. Reprint, 1972.

Steinman, D.B. *The Builders of the Bridge*. New York: Harcourt, Brace, 1945. Reprint, New York: Arno Press, 1972.

Veglahn, Nancy. *The Spider of Brooklyn Heights*. New York: Scribner, 1967.

Periodicals

Birdsall, Blair. "The Brooklyn Bridge at 100." *Technology Review* (April 1983): p. 60.

Hammill, Pete. "The Glory of the Brooklyn Bridge." *New York* (May 30, 1983): p. 27.

McCullough, David. "The Great Bridge and the American Imagination." *New York Times Magazine* (March 27, 1983): p. 28.

Wohleber, Curt. "The Bridging of America: The Roebling Saga." *American Heritage* (April 1991): p. 46.

Web Sites

"Brooklyn Bridge." *Great Buildings Online*. Basic facts about the Brooklyn Bridge. http://www.greatbuildings.com/buildings/Brooklyn_Bridge.html (accessed on March 24, 2004).

John A. Roebling's Sons Co. Online History Archive. http://www.invention factory.com/history/main.html (accessed on March 24, 2004).

O. E. Rölvaag

Born April 22, 1876
Rølvaag, Norway

Died November 5, 1931
Northfield, Minnesota

Novelist who focused on the lives of immigrants in Minnesota and South Dakota

O. E. Rölvaag is best known for his novels centered on the experiences of Norwegian Americans living in rural areas of Minnesota and South Dakota. His main characters face conflicts as they try to maintain their self-identity while adapting to new social and physical surroundings. Drawing on his own experiences, Rölvaag created many characters who welcome their new world while struggling with spiritual and cultural ties to their past.

"[There] will scarcely be a life history which it would not be interesting to look at if it were singled out for scrutiny. Human portraiture has no end."

Born in a fishing village

O. E. Rölvaag was born Ole Edvart Pedersen on April 22, 1876, one of seven children of Peder Benjamin Jakobsen and Ellerine Pedersdatter Vaag. He was born in the family's cottage in a small fishing village on the island of Dønna, near the Arctic Circle in Norway. The settlement had no official name, but it was referred to as Rølvaag, the name of a nearby cove where the fishermen kept their boats. The rough land-scape and surrounding sea inspired young Rölvaag as he dreamed of becoming a poet. As a boy, Rölvaag read books he

O. E. Rölvaag.
Bettmann/Corbis.

From Little Opportunity to a Big Decision

O. E. Rölvaag tried for three years through letters to convince an uncle who lived in South Dakota to help him immigrate to the United States. He saw little opportunity in his native land, other than a hard life as a fisherman. Finally, when Rölvaag was twenty years old in 1896, a letter from his uncle arrived. The uncle invited Rölvaag to come to America and included a ticket to cross the Atlantic Ocean by boat.

However, the owner of the fishing fleet where he worked took Rölvaag to a town one morning where a large new boat was for sale. "If you will send back that ticket to your uncle," the fishing fleet owner told Rölvaag, "I will buy [a] boat for you. You shall command her; and when she has paid for herself [brought in enough money from fishing to cover the cost of buying the boat], she shall be yours."

After believing he had a bleak future of hard work in a harsh environment, Rölvaag suddenly had two options: he could work to become a captain of his own boat, or he could travel to an uncertain future in America. He sat on a hillside and considered his options all that day. Finally, he returned to the fleet owner and said, "I'm sorry, but I cannot accept your offer. I am going to America."

Rölvaag's American life did not begin on a good note. He arrived in New York City with no money to buy food and faced a three-day train ride to South Dakota. When he arrived in South Dakota, his uncle was not there to greet him—there had been a mix-up in schedules. Speaking no English, Rölvaag wandered for two more days before he found someone who spoke Norwegian and could give him directions to his uncle's farm. When he finally reached his uncle's farm, he was warmly greeted and given a farm job. That job, however, proved to be as difficult, demanding, and uninspiring as the one he left behind in Norway.

obtained by walking several miles to use libraries that served the fishing community.

Rölvaag's formal schooling ran for nine weeks a year over seven years. His education ended when he turned fourteen and joined a fishing fleet. Attracted by opportunities in the United States that were described by immigrants in letters and during their visits back to Norway, Rölvaag wrote several letters to an uncle who had immigrated to South Dakota, asking for his help so he could go to America. His opportunity to travel to America came at about the same time he was offered the position of captain of his own boat in a fishing fleet. The twenty-year-old Rölvaag boarded a boat for New York.

Returns to school

Rölvaag traveled to Elk Point, South Dakota, where he worked on his uncle's farm, but he found it as difficult and dreary as his life as a fisherman. Encouraged by a local pastor to continue his schooling, Rölvaag left his farm job in November 1898 and traveled to Minnesota. He entered Augustana Academy in Canton, Minnesota, and changed his last name from Pedersen to Rölvaag, the name of the cove near the village where he was born. (The spelling of his name differs from that of the cove: for his name, he used the "ö" common in many European languages instead of the "ø" that is more specific to Scandinavian languages.) Augustana Academy was a preparatory school where teenagers were trained for college. Rölvaag was twenty-two when he began classes, spoke little English, and had not been in a classroom in years. But being around books again inspired him, and he soon became an excellent student. While at the Academy he met a fellow student, Jennie Marie Berdahl, who would later become his wife.

After graduating from Augustana Academy in 1901, Rölvaag enrolled at St. Olaf College, a Norwegian Lutheran school in Northfield, Minnesota. He supported himself and paid for his education by working in a kitchen, delivering wood for heating stoves, and painting buildings on campus. During his junior year, he began writing a novel, but he never completed it. To earn extra money during summers, Rölvaag went on teaching assignments to work with immigrants in Nebraska and Wyoming.

Rölvaag had opportunities to continue his studies by focusing on theology, or the study of religion, but he wanted to marry Berdahl and viewed teaching as a career through which he could support a family. Following graduation from St. Olaf, he was offered a teaching position at the college on the condition that he first spend a year studying at the University of Christiania in Norway. (The city of Christiania was renamed Oslo in 1925). His experience returning to Norway was enlightening. Rölvaag discovered that he and many other immigrants felt they did not fully belong in their new home or the one they had left behind.

Rölvaag returned to St. Olaf in the fall of 1906. He and Berdahl were married in 1908, the same year Rölvaag became a naturalized American citizen. The Rölvaags would have four children. The first child, Olaf, was born in 1909 but died at age six from illness, and the youngest, Paul, was born in 1915 but died from drowning in 1920. Two children survived to adulthood: Ella, who was born in 1910, and Karl, who was born in 1913. Karl Rölvaag would serve as governor of Minnesota from 1963 to 1967 and as ambassador to Iceland from 1967 to 1969.

Novels published

While teaching and raising a family, Rölvaag resumed writing. He had written poetry in Norway and began a novel that he never completed while at St. Olaf. His first novel, *Amerika-Breve fra P. A. Smevik til Hans Far og Bror i Norge* (1912; later translated into English and published as *The Third Life of Per Smevik* in 1971), was printed by a publisher of Norwegian books in Minneapolis, Minnesota. Rölvaag wrote it under a pseudonym, Paal Morck, because the novel was so closely based on his real-life experience and people he knew. Like Rölvaag, the novel's protagonist, or principal character, is a Norwegian fisherman who immigrates to America, travels in a strange countryside without help, and becomes disenchanted with the Americans he meets. They seem interested only in their jobs and making money. This theme is repeated in *To Tullinger: Et Billede fra Idag* (1920; revised and published as *Pure Gold* in 1930), which focuses on a couple so obsessed with material gain that they abandon the values of their heritage.

Rölvaag's next novel, *Længselens Baat: Film-billeder. Første Bok* (1921; translated as *The Boat of Longing* in 1933), on the other hand, traces the struggle of a sensitive, talented violinist who comes to America hoping to fulfill his dream of living a life where art is appreciated. The English-language edition of this novel featured a quote by Rölvaag on the cover that sums up the theme of the story: "It is a mistaken belief that the immigrant has no soul." The violinist, Nils, leaves Norway to pursue his art, but he and his friend Per struggle in hostile environments in Minneapolis slums and the Minnesota wilderness. "Chief among the hidden arguments of the novel is the contention that the 'soul' needs continuity if it is to grow," wrote Theodore Jorgenson and Nora O. Solum in *Ole Edvart Rölvaag: A Biography* (1939). "The great misfortune of Nils and Per is their rootlessness," they added. "And this rootlessness is the eternal tragedy that accompanies any migratory movement like a dark shadow."

An American best-seller

Rölvaag won national attention in the United States in 1927 when the first of a trilogy of novels was published. To prepare to begin writing what Rölvaag saw as his most ambitious project, he took a year's leave from teaching at St. Olaf in 1923 to concentrate on writing. He also benefited from long talks with his father-in-law, Andrew Berdahl, whose grandparents were early white settlers in South Dakota. Berdahl provided great historical material for Rölvaag's two-part novel, published in Norway as *I de Dage: Fortælling om Norske Nykommere i Amerika* (which translates as *In Those Days: A Story of Norwegian Immigrants in America)* in 1924 and *I de Dage: Riket Grundlægges* (which translates as *In Those Days: The Founding of the Kingdom) in 1925.*

These works were popular and critical successes in Scandanavia, which led to a feature article on Rölvaag in the *Minneapolis Journal* newspaper in 1926. It described Rölvaag as a little-known local professor who was a major literary sensation in Europe. The article was read by Lincoln Colcord (1883–1947), a journalist who had an editorial contact at a major book publisher in New York City. Colcord met Rölvaag and encouraged him to work with translators to make an English-language version of the novels. Colcord reviewed the translation and convinced his friend at the Harper Company to release the English-language version as one book, to be titled titled *Giants in the Earth.*

Published in 1927, *Giants in the Earth* was a popular and critical success in the United States, selling more than eighty thousand copies that year. The novel follows a couple of second-generation Norwegian Americans—a daring man and his timid wife—as they struggle to survive as early pioneers in the rough environment of South Dakota. The husband is obsessed with becoming prosperous through farming, while the wife grows increasingly isolated. They grow apart during a series of failures on the farm, most of which result from the harsh environment of long frigid winters and brief scalding summers.

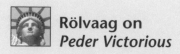
Giants in the Earth forms a trilogy with two later novels, *Peder Seier* (1928; translated into English and published as *Peder Victorious* in 1929) and *Den Signede Dag* (*Their Father's God,* 1931). The title character of *Peder Victorious* rebels against both his mother's stern religious beliefs and the local community after it shames a poor immigrant girl for having a child out of wedlock. She commits suicide. Peder's "victory" is ironic—he loses connection with his heritage in order to become more like Americans he admires.

In *Their Father's God,* Peder and his wife live on a farm begun by their parents—the protagonists of *Giants in the Earth*—that is now prosperous. When a prolonged drought threatens all the farms in the area, conflict arises between the couple and between Peder and the larger community. In his struggle to survive, Peder rediscovers the values of his Norwegian background.

Rölvaag's legacy

Rölvaag's health was failing while he was working on *Their Father's God.* He suffered several heart attacks before dying on November 5, 1931, shortly after the novel was published. The trilogy brought national recognition to Rölvaag, but he already enjoyed several other accomplishments. At St. Olaf, he developed and taught one of the first courses on immigrant history in the United States. He helped found several organizations to preserve Norwegian culture, including the Norwegian-American Historical Association, which was still active in the twenty-first century. He was Knighted (Order of St. Olav) by King Haakon VII (1872–1957) of Norway in 1926. The Ole Rölvaag Memorial Library at St. Olaf was named for him in 1944.

His enduring literary legacy prompted a new collection of his short stories, *When the Wind Is in the South and Other Stories* (1984). A documentary film, *Letters from America: The Life and Times of O. E. Rölvaag,* shot in Norway and the American Midwest, was produced with the help of Rölvaag's family and scholars of Norwegian American culture and is narrated with Rölvaag's observations. In a work reviewing the film and Rölvaag's literary work, author Peter Thaler observed that Rölvaag applauded "the financial success of Norwegian Americans, but he was dismayed at the spiritual impoverishment that seemed to accompany it. In their rush for material goods," Thaler concluded his summary of Rölvaag's view, "many immigrants discarded their cultural and spiritual traditions."

—Roger Matuz

For More Information

Books
Haugen, Einar. *Ole Edvart Rölvaag.* Boston: Twayne, 1983.

Jorgenson, Theodore, and Nora O. Solum. *Ole Edvart Rölvaag: A Biography.* New York: Harper, 1939.

Reigstad, Paul. *Rölvaag: His Life and Art.* Lincoln: University of Nebraska Press, 1972.

Rölvaag, O. E. *Giants in the Earth: A Saga of the Prairie.* New York: Harper, 1927. Multiple reprints.

Simonson, Harold P. *Prairies Within: The Tragic Trilogy of Ole Rölvaag.* Seattle: University of Washington Press, 1987.

Thaler, Peter. *Norwegian Minds, American Dreams: Ethnic Activism Among Norwegian-American Intellectuals.* Dover: University of Delaware Press, 1998.

Periodicals
Eddy, Sara. "Wheat and Potatoes': Reconstructing Whiteness in O. E. Rölvaag's Immigrant Trilogy." *MELUS: The Journal of the Society for the Study of the Multi-Ethnic Literature of the United States* (Spring 2001): pp. 129–49.

Web Sites
"Minnesota Authors Biographies Project: Ole E. Rölvaag." *Minnesota Historical Society.* http://people.mnhs.org/authors/biog_detail.cfm?PersonID=Rolv336 (accessed on March 24, 2004).

Edward Said

Born November 1, 1935
Jerusalem, Palestine

Died September 25, 2003
New York, New York

Political, social, and arts critic and commentator; contributor to Palestine's Declaration of Statehood (1988)

"Palestine is a thankless cause.... How many friends avoid the subject? How many colleagues want nothing of Palestine's controversy? How many liberals have time for Bosnia and Somalia and South Africa and Nicaragua and human and civil rights everywhere on Earth, but not for Palestine and the Palestinians?"

Edward Said. *Corbis.*

Edward Said was the most visible supporter in the United States for Palestinian people. He helped author the English-language version of the Palestine Declaration of Statehood in 1988, through which the Palestine Liberation Organization sought to establish a nation of Palestinian people. They had been without a country since 1947, living in lands occupied first by Jordan and Egypt, and then after 1967 by Israel. In 1991, however, Said resigned from his position on the Palestine National Committee because he was dissatisfied with the Palestine leadership and negotiations over statehood. By that time, Said had long distinguished himself as a literary and opera critic, television commentator, and popular public lecturer. His editorials on the Middle East appeared in major newspapers worldwide. He was also an accomplished pianist and formed the West-Eastern Divan Orchestra with Israeli Daniel Barenboim (1942–) in 1999. They shared a belief that art is limitless in its potential, unlike political ideologies.

Out of place

Edward W. Said (pronounced sah-EED) was born in

Jerusalem, Palestine, on November 1, 1935, to Wadie and Hilda Musa Said. Said's father had immigrated to the United States before World War I (1914–18). After serving with U.S. forces in France during the war, Wadie Said returned to Jerusalem. He was a wealthy businessman in writing supplies and thought of himself as a Westerner (someone from Europe or the United States; he held American citizenship). He preferred to be called William (an Americanized version of Wadie) and named his son Edward after England's prince of Wales (1894–1972). Said's mother was the daughter of a Baptist minister from Nazareth. The marriage of Said's parents was arranged (a marriage contract negotiated by parties other than both the bride and the groom).

The Said family spoke English at home, using Arabic only when speaking to servants. The mix of Western influences in a Middle Eastern environment left Said with a divided sense of identity as he grew up, as he noted in his autobiography, *Out of Place: A Memoir* (1999). He always felt that he was an outsider, as the title of his autobiography implies.

Said grew up primarily in Cairo, Egypt, where his father's business was located. The family owned property in Jerusalem, in the region that since ancient times had been called Palestine, but they were permanently exiled from Palestine after the Arab-Israeli War (1947–49). The war was fought after the United Nations (UN) divided land in the Middle East that had been occupied by Great Britain after World War I and had been called Palestine. The UN wanted to provide for two nations, Israel and Palestine (see box). The surrounding Arab nations refused to recognize the Jewish state of Israel, and a war was fought in which the Jewish people were successful. Thousands of Palestinians became refugees, or people without a homeland, following that war.

Said was educated at a private school in Cairo. In 1951, he immigrated to the United States and finished his high-school education at Mount Hermon, a private school in Massachusetts. Said graduated from Princeton University in 1957 and then went on to Harvard University. While attaining his master's degree (1960) and his doctorate in philosophy (Ph.D., 1964) from Harvard, he worked as a tutor in history and literature. He became a professor of literature at Columbia University in 1963 and continued there for over thirty years while also serving as a visiting professor at several American universities.

Political awakening

Said's first book, *Joseph Conrad and the Fiction of Autobiography* (1966), set the tone for his work as a critic of literature. Joseph Conrad (1857–1924) was born in Poland but spent much of his early life at sea, working on sailing ships and in the British Merchant Navy. He later wrote fictional works set in places he had traveled, such as Africa and the Far East. In his book on Conrad, Said argued that the author, like other Western writers, projected political dimensions in his work that represented the viewpoint of colonialists, or nations that exert control over a foreign land and impose laws and customs on the people—in effect, "civilizing" them according to standards set by the colonialists. That dimension, noted Said, should be considered when reading all Western literature.

During his twenties, Said concentrated on graduate school, teaching, literary criticism, and music; he was also an excellent pianist and became a critic on opera. His political interests were stirred after he turned thirty by the Arab-Israeli War of 1967, which Israel won and resulted in many more Palestinians losing their property. After the war in the late 1940s, Palestinians lived in lands on the west bank of the Jordan River, under the authority of Jordan, and on the Gaza strip (a strip of land between Israel and Egypt), under the authority of Egypt. After the war of 1967, those two areas fell under the control of Israel. Said began following events and became involved in the Palestinians' attempt to form a nation. Meanwhile, Said was married in 1970 to Mariam Cortas. They would have two children, Wadie and Najla. Said continue to write literary criticism while his political involvement deepened.

Joins the Palestinian cause

Said was elected to the Palestine National Council (PNC) in 1977. This group provided advice to Yasir Arafat (1929–), leader of the Palestine Liberation Organization (PLO), in his effort to win international recognition for a Palestinian

Edward Said throws a stone at Israeli soldiers on the Lebanese-Israeli border. This incident resulted in Said being barred from addressing a Sigmund Freud Society conference in Austria. *© AFP/Corbis.*

state. Unlike some members of the council who supported armed conflict with Israel, Said advocated the two-state solution (see box). Said favored recognition of Israel; Arab states and most Arab people did not at that time. After much bloodshed in the Middle East and much debate among Palestinian leaders, the policy was adopted at a PNC meeting in Algiers, Algeria, in 1988. Said drafted the English version of the Palestinian declaration of statehood. Meanwhile, he represented

Palestine in Recent History

On November 29, 1947, the United Nations voted to partition, or divide, an area of the Middle East, known historically as Palestine and which had been under the control of Great Britain since World War I, into two states, one Jewish, and one Arab. Palestinian Arabs and the surrounding Arab states rejected the partition. The Jewish population accepted it, and on May 14, 1948, they declared independence and formed the state of Israel. Armies of Egypt, Iraq, Jordan, Lebanon, and Syria invaded Israel. Large numbers of Palestinian Arabs fled during the fighting, and others were expelled from their homes. The Jewish forces prevailed, and the state of Israel was established.

The territories that were to form an Arab state in Palestine were occupied by Jordan (the West Bank) and Egypt (the Gaza Strip) from 1948 to 1967, when Israel entered those areas, defended them in the Six Day War, and occupied them afterward. Palestinians have struggled to assert their independence since then. The word "Palestine" describes a geographical area and the proposed state of the Palestinian people.

the Palestinian view in articles in American magazines and as a commentator on television news programs.

Recognition of Israel's right to exist opened the way for the United States to work with the PLO and Israel in such talks as the Madrid Conference in Spain and the Oslo Peace Process in Norway. As the peace process gained momentum, however, Said adopted an increasingly critical stance. In 1991, he resigned from the PNC, believing the Oslo declaration was more favorable to Israel. Said had come under increasingly negative criticism by Israeli supporters in the United States, and now he was criticized by Palestinian supporters as well. He became the subject of censorship by Palestinian authorities. His advocacy of Palestinian rights did not prevent him from criticizing Palestinian policies and leadership.

"Said made lots of enemies," noted an obituary that appeared in *Newsweek* magazine upon Said's death in 2003. "His searing critiques of American Middle East policy made him a bogeyman for many in the pro-Israel camp: There were demands that he be reprimanded by Columbia [University] after he threw a stone at Israel from across the Lebanese border. And yet his condemnations of Yasir Arafat, the Palestinian regime and Arab intellectuals' 'creeping, nasty wave of anti-Semitism and hypocritical righteousness' led some Arabs to denounce him as a traitor."

Exposes stereotypes

During the period from 1978 to 1991 when Said was a member of the PNC, he wrote several more books, including two that examine European and American representations of the peoples and societies of the Middle East. *Orientalism* (1978) argues that scholars, journalists, and creative writers stereotype Middle Eastern cultures as unchanging and violent. These negative depictions, Said continued, come to inform popular attitudes and then public policy toward the region and are used to justify Western economic and political domination of the Middle East. *Covering Islam: How the Media and the Experts Determine How We See the Rest of the World* (1981) points to ways Western media perpetuate stereotypes, or present the same images, often unflattering, over and over again, of Muslims and ignores the diversity of Islamic beliefs. "With *Orientalism*," wrote Habeeb Salloum, "Said transformed the way people looked at Islam, the Arabs, and the Middle East. This work, and his later book, *Culture and Imperialism* (1993), were important studies of how artistic creation and cultural prejudices converge [come together] and made him a much-sought-after lecturer in the intellectual world."

Said discussed the plight of Palestinians and the momentum building toward the declaration of statehood in 1988 in such works as *The Question of Palestine* (1979) and *After the Last Sky: Palestinian Lives* (1986). In these works, Said traced the history of the Palestinians and the Israeli-Palestinian conflict and argues that Palestinian efforts to obtain statehood have been made to appear unjustifiable by some Israeli supporters.

During the 1990s, Said continued to be outspoken, attacking what he saw as Israeli violations of the human rights of Palestinians and condemning U.S. policies in the Middle East in articles and on national television news programs. He also continued writing a music column for *The Nation* magazine and a column for the Arabic newspapers *al-Hayat* in London and *Al-Ahram* in Egypt. His articles appeared in U.S. periodicals as well as in newspapers in France, Italy, Sweden, Britain, Spain, Pakistan, India, and Japan.

Health declines

Said was diagnosed with leukemia, a form of cancer, in the early 1990s. As his health grew fragile near the end of the decade, he began focusing his energy on music. He founded the West-Eastern Divan Orchestra with Daniel Barenboim, an

Edward Said shakes hands with Jewish musician Daniel Berenboim, who along with Said founded the West-Eastern Divan Orchestra.
© Reuters/Corbis.

Israeli citizen, in 1999. With Said's assistance (Said was an accomplished pianist), Barenboim gave master classes for Palestinian students in the West Bank, which was occupied by Israel. The orchestra made a triumphant tour of Europe.

Said also wrote his autobiography, *Out of Place: A Memoir* (1999). Looking back on his youth, Said wrote, "A constant property links young Edward with the adult Said:

the notion of out of placeness, of exile, as changeless, permanent features of his personality that existed before he could have known what the future had in store for him." Said's final works included *The End of the Peace Process: Oslo and After* (2000), his reflections on why negotiations between Israel and the Palestinians failed in the 1990s; *Reflections on Exile and Other Essays* (2000), a collection of Said's writings on politics and literature; and *Power, Politics, and Culture: Interviews with Edward W. Said* (2001), a collection of interviews and panel discussions involving Said from the years 1976 to 2000.

"*Power, Politics, and Culture* covers a wide range of topics, including the Palestinian-Israeli conflict and the peace process, the Gulf War, Middle East politics, literary criticism, cultural theory, opera, and travel drawn from a variety of publications, both in the United States and abroad," noted Habeeb Salloum in *Contemporary Review*. Upon Said's death in 2003, Salloum said, "His political activism and his enormous on-going contributions to humanities, as well as his wide-ranging intellectual life for many years aroused passionate feelings, pro and con, among his readers." Salloum added, "He appealed to a large constituency of devotees throughout the world who regarded him as a paragon [model of excellence] of intellectuals."

—Roger Matuz

For More Information

Books

Marrouchi, Mustapha. *Edward Said at the Limits*. Albany: State University of New York Press, 2004.

Said, Edward W. *The Edward Said Reader*. Edited by Moustafa Bayoumi and Andrew Rubin. New York: Vintage Books, 2000.

Said, Edward W. *Out of Place: A Memoir*. New York: Knopf, 1999.

Periodicals

"Edward Said: Appreciation of Writer, Teacher, Music Critic and Contributor to *The Nation*; Critic of Western Imperialism and Champion of Palestinian Liberation" (obituary). *The Nation* (October 20, 2003): p. 4.

Salloum, Habeeb. "Edward Said: The Palestinian Intellectual Champion." *Contemporary Review* (November 2003): pp. 271–74.

"A Scholar and Exile: Edward Said" (obituary). *Newsweek International* (October 6, 2003): p. 60.

Web Sites

The Edward Said Archive. http://www.edwardsaid.org/modules/news/ (accessed on March 24, 2004).

Ruthven, Malise. "Edward Said: Controversial Literary Critic and Bold Advocate of the Palestinian Cause in America" (obituary). *The Guardian* (September 26, 2003). http://www.guardian.co.uk/israel/Story/0,2763,1049931,00.html (accessed on March 24, 2004).

Arnold Schwarzenegger

Born July 30, 1947
Graz, Austria

Governor of California, movie star, and champion bodybuilder

"For the people to win, politics *as usual* must lose."

"**D**o we want philosophy or action? I want action." Arnold Schwarzenegger made that statement in reply to a question posed by a journalist about whether an after-school program he championed would put the government in the position of replacing moms. The statement reflects Schwarzenegger's style: He sets a goal and works tirelessly and aggressively toward it, adding charm and a knack for self-promotion as he undertakes quests for ultimate titles: he has been Mr. Universe, King of the Box Office, Chairman of the President's Council on Physical Fitness, and Governor of California. Schwarzenegger has been an action hero in movies and in real life.

Working out

Arnold Alois Schwarzenegger was born on July 30, 1947, in Graz, Austria, and raised in the nearby village of Thal. His father, Gustav, was a police officer. Austria at the time was still recovering from the effects of World War II (1939–45) and having been occupied by Nazi Germany, a regime, led by

Arnold Schwarzenegger.
© *Kenneth James/Corbis.*

Adolf Hitler (1889–1945), known primarily for its brutal policies of racism. The Schwarzenegger family, which included mother Aurelia and older brother Meinhard, struggled to survive a time of scarcity and slow rebuilding. The family lacked indoor plumbing and a refrigerator until Arnold was a teenager. Schwarzenegger's father was a strict disciplinarian. He woke his sons shortly after sunrise to begin their morning chores. After chores, the boys performed an exercise routine before eating a breakfast meal planned by their father.

The Schwarzeneggers enjoyed sports. Schwarzenegger's father often pitted his two sons in competitions. Arnold was younger and often lost these competitions, which contributed to the psychological drive that led to his achievements as an adult. Schwarzenegger's father excelled at curling, an ice sport where players take turns directing their curling stones to a target area. Meinhard was a champion boxer; he died in an automobile accident at the age of twenty-three. Arnold played soccer as a child and advanced at age twelve to a senior level team, the Graz Athletic Club.

When his soccer coach took the team to a gym to work out with weights to improve their strength and stamina, Schwarzenegger discovered he enjoyed the workouts. Around that time, he met Kurt Marnul, a professional bodybuilder who invited Schwarzenegger to train at the Athletic Union in Graz. By the age of fifteen, Schwarzenegger was studying anatomy and developing training routines to maximize the results of his hard work. Worried about his son's obsession with weightlifting (Schwarzenegger's father called it "Austria's least favorite sport"), his father limited Schwarzenegger's trips to the athletic club. Schwarzenegger responded by building a makeshift gym at home that would allow him to continue his training.

After graduating from high school in 1965, Schwarzenegger enlisted in the Austrian army. The regimentation of army life was not new to him, having lived under the strict discipline enforced by his father. When he was free from duty, which included driving a tank, Schwarzenegger continued the strenuous training regimen he had devised. Meanwhile, the army diet—emphasizing meat and foods rich in protein—helped Schwarzenegger bulk up his physique. His exercise routine transformed bulk into thick muscle. After just one month of military service, Schwarzenegger entered and won his first bodybuilding title, Mr. Junior Europe, in Stuttgart, Germany. A bit too eager to compete, Schwarzenegger had left his military base without permission to compete in Stuttgart. Upon his return, he was sentenced to a military jail for having been absent without leave.

Upon his release from military jail, Schwarzenegger initiated his new plan that concentrated on powerlifting, a quicker, and more strenuous type of weightlifting. He won the Austrian Junior Olympic Powerlifting championship, but in the process he realized that the stress of powerlifting would eventually wear him out rather than build up his body. He returned to a bodybuilding program with daily sessions running for several hours.

Mr. Universe

In 1967, Schwarzenegger won the first of his five titles in the Mr. Universe competition. Playing off his dominating performance that earned him the top bodybuilding prize, Schwarzenegger founded a business through which he could operate in a variety of functions, from investing in real estate to supplying gyms with equipment and developing diet products. In 1968, Schwarzenegger made his first visit to the United States to attend the Mr. Universe competition in Miami, Florida. Schwarzenegger lost his title, but finished second. Nevertheless, fitness pioneer Joe Weider (1922–) was impressed by Schwarzenegger and invited him to Los Angeles to train under his sponsorship.

Weider provided Schwarzenegger with an apartment, a car, and a weekly salary. In exchange, Schwarzenegger contributed articles on the training methods he developed to Weider's bodybuilding magazines, including *Muscle and Fitness*. In Los Angeles, Schwarzenegger devoted himself almost

 Schwarzenegger's Early Experiences with Bodybuilding

In an excerpt from *Arnold: The Education of a Bodybuilder*, Arnold Schwarzenegger recalls his early love of bodybuilding:

During the early years I didn't care how I felt about anything except bodybuilding. It consumed every minute of my days and all my best effort.... When I was ten years old I got this thing that I wanted to be the best in swimming, so I started swimming. I won championships, but I felt I couldn't be the best. I tried it in skiing, but there I felt that I didn't have the potential. I played soccer, but I didn't like that too well because there I didn't get the credit alone if I did something special. Then I started weight lifting through other sports.... I won the Austrian championship in 1964 but I found out I was just too tall. So I quit that and went into bodybuilding. Two years later I found out that that's it—that's what I can be best in.

exclusively to training, intent on recapturing the Mr. Universe crown. Schwarzenegger proceeded to dominate the sport. He won six consecutive Mr. Olympia contests in addition to winning back the Mr. Universe title and adding three more to his total. He retired from bodybuilding competitions in 1975, except for a brief comeback in 1980 to take his seventh and final Mr. Olympia title. By then, he had created many other opportunities to pursue.

"I'll be back"

Living in Los Angeles and accustomed to performing before audiences and cameras, Schwarzenegger began to pursue an acting career. As early as 1970, when Schwarzenegger was twenty-two, his physique made him ideal for the title role in a low-budget Italian television production, *Hercules Goes to New York*. Schwarzenegger had a small role in *The Long Goodbye,* a 1973 film by acclaimed director Robert Altman (1925–). In 1975, Schwarzenegger played bodybuilder Joe Santos in the film *Stay Hungry,* for which he won a Golden Globe award for best new actor. *Pumping Iron* (1977), his next film, is a documentary on body building, following several world-class bodybuilders as they prepare for competition— from working out in gyms to participation in a contest. *Pumping Iron* is an "extraordinary documentary of Schwarzenegger's rise in the nascent [emerging] bodybuilding culture of the time," wrote Andrew Sullivan in *Time* magazine more than twenty-five years after the film was released. "He took a minor and largely derided [ridiculed] sport and made it a world-wide sensation," Sullivan added.

In 1978, Schwarzenegger met television journalist Maria Shriver (1955–). They were married in 1986 and would have four children. Shriver is the daughter of R. Sargent Shriver (1915–), former director of the Peace Corps and the running mate of 1972 Democratic presidential candidate George McGovern (1922–), and Eunice Kennedy Shriver, sister of the late U.S. president John F. Kennedy (1917–1963; served 1961–63). Schwarzenegger's extended family, the Kennedy clan, had produced many prominent politicians. Schwarzenegger would later become a politician himself, and he shared some of the Kennedy family's activism for social programs to assist those in need. But Schwarzenegger would be elected as a Republican, not as a Democrat, of which the Kennedys are powerful symbols.

In addition to politics, Shriver also introduced Schwarzenegger to one of her favorite causes, the Special Olympics. This organization provides opportunities for physically challenged children to play and compete in sports. Schwarzenegger eagerly joined the group and brought increasingly greater attention to it as he himself became an increasingly famous public figure.

During the 1980s, Schwarzenegger emerged as one of the most popular and bankable of movie stars. He was an obvious choice to play the lead in the film versions of Conan, a muscular sword-and-sorcery hero whose adventures were related in a series of books. What *Conan the Barbarian* (1982) and *Conan the Destroyer* (1984) lacked in artistry and acting was more than made up for in box-office success. More significant was Schwarzenegger's role as a violent cyborg (a bionic, or electromechanical, human) sent from the future to eliminate the mother of mankind's future leader in *The Terminator* (1984). In this film, Schwarzenegger created a screen persona that minimized his need for acting skills; his characters became larger-than-life, caught up in fast-paced life and death situations. They also maintained a disarming charm, spouting tough one-liners that fans enjoyed repeating. Schwarzenegger himself enjoys repeating his trademark line from *The Terminator:* "I'll be back."

A series of highly popular action films followed—*Commando* (1985), *Raw Deal* (1986), *The Running Man* (1987), and *Predator* (1987). In 1988, Schwarzenegger expanded into comic roles, which also met with box-office success. In *Twins* (1988), the tall, muscular Schwarzenegger played the unlikely fraternal twin of the short, chubby actor Danny DeVito (1944–). *Kindergarten Cop* (1990) had Schwarzenegger struggling to keep peace among a group of lively kids while chasing a criminal.

Arnold Schwarzenegger plays the title role in the film *The Terminator*. Kobal Collection.

Arnold Schwarzenegger
(left) talks with President
George Bush. *AP/World Wide
Photos.*

Chairman of President's Council on Physical Fitness and Sports

Just as Schwarzenegger had been successful expanding from a career in bodybuilding to one as an actor, and from a powerful action-hero to more comic roles, he used his Hollywood popularity to bring attention to important causes. In 1990, President George Bush (1924–; served 1989–93) named Schwarzenegger chairman of the President's Council on Physical Fitness and Sports. Schwarzenegger campaigned across the fifty states to change American attitudes about fitness. He contributed an essay to *Newsweek* magazine in which he called poor physical fitness among children "America's secret tragedy."

Schwarzenegger continued to be involved with the Special Olympics and added roles as a promoter of the Inner City Games and diverse charities devoted to caring for sick children. Schwarzenegger coauthored *Arnold's Fitness for Kids: A Guide to Health, Nutrition and Exercise,* three books each directed toward a specific age group. The guides provide advice on good eating habits and emphasize play over competition.

Throughout the 1990s, Schwarzenegger continued his activism on behalf of fitness and health and continued to make popular action movies while mixing in occasional comedies. His action-hero films of the 1990s included *The Terminator, T2* (1991), *Last Action Hero* (1993), *True Lies* (1994), and *Eraser* (1996). Meanwhile, in *Junior* (1994), he played a pregnant man. Schwarzenegger became Hollywood's best-paid villain with the role of Mr. Freeze in *Batman and Robin* (1997), for which he reaped $25 million. Schwarzenegger seemed to be losing his box-office clout by 2000 with *End of Days* (2000) and *Collateral Damage* (2002). By then, however, he was transforming himself into a new role: that of politician.

Governor Arnold

Schwarzenegger's popularity as a film star made politicians want to seek him out for support. But just as he had been a self-made man in business, bodybuilding, and even in film as an action hero, Schwarzenegger took it upon himself to become a viable political force. That was most apparent in his tireless work in support of Proposition 49, an initiative to increase California state funds for before- and after-school programs that provide tutoring, homework assistance, and educational enrichment. (A proposition is a proposed law, expenditure, or other government action that is put before voters, not elected officials, to decide.)

Schwarzenegger personally delivered to the Los Angeles county clerk's office petitions bearing 750,000 signatures in support of the ballot initiative to fund California after-school programs. "Half of all California kids are now in single working-parent homes or homes with two working parents," he told Karen Kornbluh of *Washington Monthly* magazine. "One million kids under the age of 15 are home alone after school. These are kids that do not have anyone to do homework with them, take them to the sports field, or hug them," Schwarzenegger added. "Sixty percent of Californians support Schwarzenegger's proposal, which is backed by 100 mayors and a broad array of groups from the right and the left, including the California Teachers

Arnold Schwarzenegger,
with his wife Maria Shriver,
is sworn in as governor of
California by that state's
chief justice, Ronald George.
AP/World Wide Photos.

Association, the California State Sheriffs' Association, and the Howard Jarvis Taxpayers Association," noted Kornbluh. "The real mystery, then," she wondered, "isn't why Arnold is on the case. It's why more politicians aren't."

The proposition passed in a 2002 statewide election. Schwarzenegger's tireless promotion helped win the vote. Some commentators noted that self-promotion for Schwarzenegger was part of the deal. When Schwarzenegger eagerly embraced a recall vote against California governor Gray Davis (1942–) in 2003, those commentators seemed accurate. California had huge financial problems, and Davis, who was reelected in 2002, was a popular target of blame. When the initiative to recall Davis received enough petition signatures, the recall option was put to California voters in 2003. They could vote to recall Davis, and also select someone to replace him.

Schwarzenegger had been particularly aggressive in criticizing Davis. Once the recall election was official,

Schwarzenegger used his muscle as a celebrity to find a widely visible forum to announce his candidacy—*The Tonight Show with Jay Leno*. In a remarkably quick rise, Schwarzenegger helped convince California voters to recall Davis, and at the same time elect himself as the new governor.

Even as he celebrated another remarkable success in another field, Schwarzenegger understood the challenge had just begun. He had promised voters that he would not participate in politics as usual, and politicians are rarely compared with action heroes. As he told the voters, concerned about California's financial mess, "For the people to win, politics *as usual* must lose." Defeating "politics as usual" will indeed require heroic action. As Schwarzenegger noted, "This is a new political environment. This is the first time California has had an Austrian-born Mr. Universe as governor."

—*Roger Matuz*

For More Information

Books

Andrews, Nigel. *True Myths: The Life and Times of Arnold Schwarzenegger, from Pumping Iron to Governor of California*. Rev. ed. London: Bloomsbury, 2004.

Flynn, John. *The Films of Arnold Schwarzenegger*. New York: Citadel Press, 1996.

Lipsyte, Robert. *Arnold Schwarzenegger: Hercules in America*. New York: Harpercollins Juvenile Books, 1993.

Periodicals

"Arnie! Arnie! California Politics." *The Economist* (October 11, 2003): p. 30.

Kornbluh, Karen. "The Parent Gap: What Arnold Schwarzenegger Can Teach Politicians about Winning Swing Voters." *Washington Monthly* (October 2002): pp. 13–18.

Rohrer, Anneliese. "A Boy from Graz." *New York Times* (October 9, 2003): p. A37.

Schwarzenegger, Arnold, with Douglas Kent Hall. *Arnold: The Education of a Bodybuilder*. New York: Simon and Schuster, 1977.

Sullivan, Andrew. "Pumping Irony: Despite the Caricatures, Arnold May Be the Model of a New Kind of Politician." *Time* (October 20, 2003): p. 88.

Web Sites

Arnold Schwarzenegger Official Site. http://www.schwarzenegger.com/en (accessed on March 24, 2004).

"Arnold Schwarzenegger: The People's Governor." *Welcome to California.* http://www.governor.ca.gov/ (accessed on March 24, 2004).

John Shalikashvili

Born June 27, 1936
Warsaw, Poland

Military leader;
chairman of the Joint Chiefs of Staff

G eneral John Shalikashvili was the first person born outside the United States to serve as chairman of the Joint Chiefs of Staff. The chairman of this group of military commanders is the lead advisor to the president. "General Shali," as President Bill Clinton (1946–; served 1993–2001) referred to him when announcing Shalikashvili's appointment, served in the U.S. military for almost forty years. He was commissioned as an officer in 1959, served in the Vietnam War (1954–75), commanded the airlift of food to Kurdish refugees in Iraq after the Persian Gulf War (1991), and played a significant role in peace negotiations among warring factions, or groups, of the former Yugoslavia during the 1990s. "Only in America," he said upon his retirement as a four-star general in 1997, "could a foreign-born young man with a thick accent and almost unpronounceable last name get drafted into the Army as a private … and leave as the nation's highest-ranking military officer."

From Poland to Peoria

John Malchase David Shalikashvili was born on June 27, 1936, in Warsaw, Poland. He was one of three children of

"The Polish underground occupied our apartment, and shortly after that the Germans bombed it. With our apartment destroyed, we lived by just moving around.… We survived by going from cellar to cellar. Most often the only way to get anyplace was through the sewer lines.… A piece of bread during this period was like a holiday meal."

John Shalikashvili.
© Markowitz Jeffrey/
Corbis Sygma.

347

Dimitri Shalikashvili and Maria Ruediger. His mother was the daughter of a general who served the under czar, or emperor, of Russia. Shalikashvili's father was from Georgia, one of the countries ruled by Russia. He received training at a Russian military academy and fought as a cavalry officer in the Russian Civil War (1918–21). After the fall of the czarist armies to communists forces in 1917, Shalikashvili's parents both fled their homes and moved to Warsaw, where they met and were later married.

Shalikashvili's father was serving as a contract, or foreign national, officer in the Polish army when World War II (1939–45) began. Poland was invaded by and surrendered to Germany. Dimitri Shalikashvili joined a military unit composed of Georgian expatriates, or those living in a foreign land, who believed they could free their homeland from the Soviet Union by aligning themselves with Germany. But the unit was transferred to France when the American forces landed there in 1944. Shalikashvili's father was wounded, captured by the British, and moved to a prisoner-of-war camp in northern Italy.

Meanwhile, Shalikashvili's mother and the three children lived in Warsaw, in an area that was relatively peaceful until German soldiers moved in to confront an uprising of Warsaw underground forces, or civilians who work against an occupying army. "It's very difficult to describe the level of misery and destruction in Warsaw in those late summer days of 1944," Shalikashvili later told the *Peoria Journal Star* newspaper. "The Polish underground occupied our apartment, and shortly after that the Germans bombed it. With our apartment destroyed, we lived by just moving around.... We survived by going from cellar to cellar. Most often the only way to get anyplace was through the sewer lines." He added, "A piece of bread during this period was like a holiday meal." After the uprising was stopped, the Shalikashvilis were among many civilians evacuated to camps along the border between Poland and Germany. Warsaw was the most heavily damaged city in World War II.

Near the end of the war, when Soviet forces moved across Poland toward Germany, the family fled Poland, hiding in a cattle car in a train just ahead of the Soviet army. The train was attacked by planes, and the family had to scatter into nearby woods for protection. They made their way to

Pappenheim, Germany, where Maria Shalikashvili had wealthy relatives who provided the family with a place to stay. In 1946, more than a year after the war, the family was reunited with their father, who had been released from a prisoner-of-war camp in northern Italy.

In 1952, the Shalikashvilis immigrated to Peoria, Illinois, where a distant relative lived. The sixteen-year-old Shalikashvili spoke Polish, German, and Russian, and in Peoria he became proficient in English by watching John Wayne (1907–1979) movies at a local theater. He graduated with honors from Peoria High School in 1954. He went on to Bradley University, where he graduated in 1958 with a degree in mechanical engineering.

Enjoys army life

In Peoria, Shalikashvili's father worked for Central Illinois Light Company, and his mother was a file clerk at Commercial National Bank. After completing his degree at Bradley, Shalikashvili planned to work for Hyster Lift Truck Company in Peoria. Instead, his draft notice arrived in the mail. Shalikashvili completed basic training and was accepted in Officer Candidate School (OCS) at Fort Sill, Oklahoma. He was commissioned a second lieutenant in 1959 and assigned to a military base in Alaska. It was there that Shalikashvili realized he enjoyed army life. "I don't want to sound corny, but it was a life that had some kind of meaning. It wasn't just making a buck. You were doing something for your country. For me, that meant twice as much as most, because I feel I owe this country so much."

Shalikashvili decided to make a career in the army. He served as an instructor (1961 to 1963) and a staff officer (1963 to 1964) at the Army Air Defense School and Center in Fort Bliss, Texas, where he was promoted to captain in 1963. He moved to Germany in 1965 to serve with the U.S. Army Air Defense Command from 1965 to 1967, and he was promoted to major. In 1966, he married Joan E. Zimpelman. The couple would have one son.

In January 1968, Shalikashvili began serving in Vietnam. The United States had begun sending military advisors there in 1961 to help South Vietnam withstand a communist takeover from North Vietnam. Beginning in 1965, American troops were sent to Vietnam to fight in the war, and by 1967 more than five hundred thousand American troops were stationed there. Shalikashvili served as senior advisor with the responsibilities of training Vietnamese militia units, or small, civilian fighting groups, and accompany them into combat. He also worked with local officials on such projects as producing and distributing rice and organizing elections. Shalikashvili's units withstood artillery attacks and performed bravely. He was awarded the Bronze Star for valor, or bravery, for his service in Vietnam.

After leaving Vietnam in mid-1969, Shalikashvili studied at the Naval War College and at George Washington University, where he was awarded a master's degree in international relations in 1970. Over the next twenty years, he concentrated on strategic planning in the classroom and in a variety of assignments. He was in South Korea in 1971 and 1972, was promoted to lieutenant colonel in 1974, and served as commander of the First Battalion, 84th Field Artillery, from 1975 to 1977 at Fort Lewis, Washington. He was at the Army War College from 1977 to 1978 before a two-year stint in Italy, where he was promoted to colonel in 1979. From 1980 to 1981, he commanded the division artillery of the First Armored Division, U.S. Army, Europe, in Germany. In 1983, he was promoted to brigadier general, then to major general in 1986. In between two more tours of duty in Germany, he had duty in the Pentagon as the army's director of strategy, plans, and policy from 1986 to 1987. He returned to Germany in 1989 as deputy commander-in-chief, U.S. Army, Europe.

Shalikashvili was in Germany when the Persian Gulf War began and ended in a matter of weeks in early 1991. An international coalition led by the United States liberated Kuwait, which had been invaded by Iraq. Within Iraq, many people of the Kurdish ethnic group were forced from their home area in the north to harsh mountainous terrain that forms the borders of Iraq, Iran, and Turkey. An international relief expedition called Operation Provide Comfort was organized, with Shalikashvili as commander. Military units and medical personnel from the United States and a dozen other countries began entering the area in April 1991. The Operation was a success, providing humanitarian aid and establishing a safe haven for Kurds. Shalikashvili was a model com-

mander, showing diplomatic skills and military strategy to organize thirty-five thousand men and women from thirteen countries to help Kurdish refugees leave the mountains and resettle in secure zones in Iraq. "We had reports indicating that 1,000 or more of these refugees were dying each night from the weather and other problems," Shalikashvili said. "We set ourselves a goal of getting them out by June," he continued. "And we did it. In the end, we brought home some 700,000.... But we can only guess how many died."

Joint Chiefs chairman John Shalikashvili leads a military press conference in 1994.
© Markowitz Jeffrey/Corbis Sygma.

"O.K., then it's you"

After the successful mission in Iraq, Shalikashvili reported to the Pentagon in August 1991 as assistant to General Colin Powell (1937–), chairman of the Joint Chiefs of Staff (also known as the "Joint Chiefs") under President George Bush (1924–; served 1989–93). The following June, Shalikashvili became Supreme Allied Commander of Europe (SACEUR) and

Unassuming Leader

On two occasions, General Colin Powell, chairman of the Joint Chiefs of Staff, recommended Shalikashvili for promotion. Twice, Shalikashvili tried to turn the jobs down. "I recommended him for SACEUR [supreme allied commander of Europe]," Powell told *Peoria Journal Star* newspaper. "That's a pre-eminent [most important] job that normally went to a veteran four-star general. Shali was a three-star then. But he was considered the best man for the job. So he was jumped over the other candidates." Shalikashvili would urge then-president George Bush not to consider him. "I thought it was bad precedent," Shalikashvili said. "Never in our history has a three-star general been promoted to a four-star general and his first job be supreme allied commander of NATO. After all, this is the job [General Dwight] Eisenhower had."

Powell would also recommend Shalikashvili to replace him as chairman in 1993. Again, Shalikashvili had to be convinced to take the position. "I felt that I could better serve my country in Europe.... There was a second reason, too. I didn't want to follow Colin Powell. I didn't want to be reading in the papers for four years: 'He's OK, but he's no Colin Powell.'"

President Bill Clinton told Shalikashvili that he would respect his wishes not to be named chairman of the Joint Chiefs. Before Shalikashvili could return to NATO headquarters, the president called him back for a second interview. "So I went back to the White House to again explain why I didn't want the job," Shalikashvili told the *Peoria Journal Star*. "But there was a point when I told the president that if he really wanted me to do the job, I would give it my best effort. And he said, 'OK, then it's you.'"

head of the North Atlantic Treaty Organization (NATO) forces. (Ten European nations, the United States, and Canada formed NATO after World War II to ensure stability in Europe.) Shalikashvili was promoted to four-star general. His mission included preparing NATO for possible operation in Bosnia in the former nation of Yugoslavia, where genocide, or the killing of people based on their ethnic or racial origin, was occurring.

General Shalikashvili was in charge of NATO when the decision was made to threaten air strikes in Bosnia. Those threats became reality in late February 1994, marking the first time NATO used force in defense of a country outside NATO membership. Shalikashvili had to transform NATO, which was formed to defend Europe against the Soviet Union, to mobilize quickly against trouble spots, like Bosnia. (The Soviet Union had collapsed in the late 1980s and early 1990s.)

In August 1993, Shalikashvili was chosen to become chairman of the Joint Chiefs by President Bill Clinton. When he was first asked by Clinton, Shalikashvili declined, feeling his mission with NATO was incomplete. During a second discussion with the president, Shalikashvili recalled, "There was a point when I told the president that if he really wanted me to do the job, I would give it my best effort. And he said, 'OK, then it's you.'"

Shalikashvili took the position at a time of realignment in international affairs following the collapse of the Soviet Union and budget cutbacks at home. He was also succeeding General Colin Powell, a popular military leader.

During his time as chairman of the Joint Chiefs, Shalikashvili oversaw the 1994 invasion of Haiti to reinstate the elected president, Jean-Bertrand Aristide (1953–), and then transferred peacekeeping duties to a United Nations force. During the Dayton Peace Accords to address the war in Bosnia, he ensured that the military would be represented to set clear goals and objectives for a military mission. He continued the simultaneous downsizing and technological upgrading of U.S. military forces begun under General Powell.

Shalikashvili faced many international issues. Nations in Africa collapsed and Americans had to be evacuated. The administration confronted North Korea about its program to develop nuclear weapons. The confrontation was resolved diplomatically when North Korea agreed to disassemble its nuclear reactor. China and Taiwan were in a diplomatic conflict. Meanwhile, Shalikashvili advocated technological upgrading of the armed forces; for maintaining strong alliances throughout the world and enlargement of NATO; and he developed Joint Vision 2010, a conceptual framework in which all U.S. military services would plan together.

Retires from military

As President Clinton planned his second term in office in 1997, Shalikashvili announced his retirement from the military at the age of sixty. Traditionally, the chairman of the Joint Chiefs serves two two-year terms. At his retirement ceremony in 1997 at Fort Myer, Virginia, Secretary of Defense William Cohen (1940–) said that Shalikashvili's four-year tenure as chairman "was the job of responding to threats while shaping the world for the better, bringing more democracy to more nations, more stability to more regions, and thus more security to our nation." Following his retirement, Shalikashvili lectured on international studies at Stanford University. He was awarded the Medal of Honor, the nation's highest military citation, by President Clinton in 2000.

—*Roger Matuz*

For More Information

Books

Dreifus, Claudia. *Interview.* New York: Seven Stories Press, 1999.

Shalikashvili, John, and Stanley R. Sloan. *NATO, the European Union, and the Atlantic Community.* New York: Rowman & Littlefield, 2002.

Periodicals

Goldstein, Lyle J. "General John Shalikashvili and the Civil-Military Relations of Peacekeeping." *Armed Forces & Society* (Fall 2000): pp. 387–411.

Weiner, Tim. "Four-Star Military Mind: John Malchase David Shalikashvili." *New York Times* (August 12, 1993): p. A22.

Web Sites

"General John Malchase David Shalikashvili." *The Army Historical Foundation.* http://www.armyhistoryfnd.org/armyhist/research/detail2.cfm?webpage_id=144&page_type_id=3 (accessed on March 26, 2004).

"Newsmaker Interview with General John Shalikashvili." *Online NewsHour.* http://www.pbs.org/newshour/bb/bosnia/bosnia_1-5.html (accessed on March 26, 2004).

"Shalikashvili: A Peorian in the Pentagon." *Journal Star Online Special Edition: The Legacy Project.* http://www.pjstar.com/services/special/legacyproject/shalikashvili.html (accessed on March 26, 2004).

Samuel Slater

**Born June 9, 1768
Belper, England**

**Died April 20, 1835
Webster, Rhode Island**

**Industrialist who brought secret designs
of early textile machinery to
the United States**

When Samuel Slater landed in the United States in 1789, he brought with him detailed plans to make automated machinery used to spin yarn from cotton, equipment that was a key element in launching the Industrial Revolution in the United States. The Industrial Revolution is the historical process of replacing traditional hand-crafted methods of manufacturing with complex machinery using energy sources besides muscle power, such as steam engines or waterwheels. Slater did not pack the plans in his baggage, which would have violated English law. He brought the designs in his head. After years of working with industrial equipment in England, he had memorized the thousands of details of how the machines worked. The United States at the time was eager to build textile factories similar to the ones that were changing the face of the British economy. Slater became known as the father of the American Industrial Revolution, and he started a string of successful textile factories in New England.

Growing up in England

Samuel Slater was born on a farm near the town of Belper, England. His father, William Slater, was a prosperous

"I understand you have taught us how to spin."

U.S. president Andrew Jackson, who called Slater "father of American manufactures"

Samuel Slater. *Library of Congress.*

Richard Arkwright, inventor of a yarn-spinning machine.

farmer who also bought and sold land to make money. In the early 1880s, William Slater sold a piece of land that included a stream running through it to Jedediah Strutt (1726–1797), a prominent business owner. Strutt planned to build a factory on Slater's land, taking advantage of the rushing water to propel a waterwheel and thereby provide power to automated textile manufacturing equipment. Strutt was an early pioneer in the establishment of new factories that housed machinery capable of doing the work of skilled craftsmen, but much faster and with fewer people. The process of substituting machines for human hands, called the Industrial Revolution, was initially concentrated in the textile industry. One set of new machines spun cotton fibers into yarn or thread; another set wove the yarn into fabric. Strutt was a partner of Richard Arkwright (1732–1792), who had invented a yarn-spinning machine that used a waterwheel pushed by a stream of water to generate the motion of the machine. Buildings that housed water-powered machines, along with the machinery inside, were called mills.

As part of the arrangement to sell his land, William Slater arranged for his son Samuel to be employed in the new factory as an apprentice, a young person who is learning the business, for the standard term of seven years. Strutt had originally wanted another son of Slater as an apprentice, but eventually chose Samuel because of the boy's ability in arithmetic. At age fourteen, Samuel Slater started working full-time, learning all aspects of the textile business—how the machinery worked, how to manage workers, and how to sell the finished products. His apprenticeship was highly successful. Slater was a clever student and became a top assistant to Strutt, even living in his boss's house. As a young man, Slater was not only put in charge of building and maintaining machinery at other mills owned by Strutt and Arkwright but was also expected to deal with the employees who worked at the mill. By the time he was twenty, Slater had a thorough knowledge of how to build and operate a textile mill.

Bringing his secrets to the United States

As successful as he was, at the end of his apprenticeship, when he was twenty-one, Slater concluded that the textile industry had a limited future in England, since men like Strutt and Arkwright had already set up dozens of factories. He worried that there were so many textile mills built in England that the industry would become overcrowded and lead to company failures. At the same time, businessmen in the newly independent United States were offering rewards for people who would bring the secrets of how to build the new factories across the Atlantic as well as employment offers for the people with skills to run them. Having already seen the business advantages of the new factories, American investors, or people with money to spend building businesses, wanted to establish American factories that could compete with those being built in England.

A spinning frame designed by Richard Arkwright.
© *Bettmann/Corbis.*

But importing a factory to the United States was not easily done. In an effort to preserve the advantages of industrialization for England, the British government had declared it illegal to export the industrial machines like Arkwright's or for skilled workers like Slater to leave the country with the secrets of industrialization in their heads.

Having decided that he had a more promising future in the United States than in England, in 1789 Samuel Slater secretly made plans to cross the Atlantic. To avoid the ban on skilled workers leaving England, he did not even tell his mother that he intended to immigrate to the United States. Dressing as a farmer to disguise himself, and hiding the certificate he had received as an apprentice, Slater boarded a ship bound for Philadelphia, Pennsylvania.

After arrival in the United States, Slater made his way to New York City where he got a job at the New York Manufacturing Company, a small textile mill. But Slater was disappointed with the company's poor equipment and its lack of a location near running water. So when he heard that Moses Brown (1738–1836), a Quaker businessman in Pawtucket, Rhode Island, near Providence, and his partner William Almy (1761–1836) were experimenting with textile machinery, Slater went to visit Brown. Almy and Brown had built a textile mill but could not get it working properly. Slater quickly identified how the equipment could be improved and offered to work for Brown and Almy. For three months, Slater made improvements to the installed machinery to make it more like the equipment designed by Arkwright. The results were so satisfactory that Brown and Almy offered to make Slater a partner in their business.

The initial spinning mill set up by Slater was a tiny operation, run by Slater and a staff of nine children between ages seven and twelve. Despite its small size, no one doubted the success of the operation, and in 1793 Slater, Brown, and Almy built a larger textile mill in Pawtucket. That factory, called Slater's Mill, was the first of several mills that Slater would eventually construct and own in New England.

Success in New England
New England made an ideal location for mills like Slater's. The region had many streams that could drive waterwheels. The streams fed into rivers that led to port cities on the Atlantic, where ships could deliver raw materials and carry off the finished goods to growing markets in big cities up and down the East Coast of the United States. At the same time, factory owners found a source of employees on New England farms. The region's rocky soil made farming difficult, and many farmers and their families were willing to exchange a life of agriculture for a life working in a factory.

One of Slater's major contributions to early American industry, aside from bringing knowledge of how to build the machinery, was his method of organizing workers, which later became known as the Rhode Island System. In his system, in addition to a factory, or mill, Slater also built housing for the workers within a short walk of their jobs. Slater pro-

One of Samuel Slater's many cotton mills in New England in 1881; this one is in Webster, Massachusetts.
© Bettmann/Corbis.

vided stores that sold food and every other necessity for the workers. Wages were paid in the form of credit at the store, helping save cash for the investors in the factory. Slater also built churches and schools near the mills; in both church and school, lessons were taught with the approval of Slater—lessons that helped reinforce attitudes among workers that contributed to the mill's success, as Slater saw it.

The Rhode Island System put into the mill owner's hands virtually every detail of the workers' lives: the hours they worked, the physical conditions inside the factory, the pay levels. When workers were hard to find, Slater and other factory owners improved conditions to make work more attractive; when there were many workers available, conditions tended to decline. Nevertheless, in the years when Slater and other pioneers in American industry were building the early mills, the standard of living usually improved for people who left their small farms to work in a mill, which is not to say that factory life was easy. Work in the factory started before sunrise and ended after sunset. The machines created dust from the cotton fibers, which could lead to respiratory diseases. The mills were cold in the winter, hot in the summer. Air conditioning was unheard of. The rapidly moving machines posed a potential danger to fingers and hands.

Expansion

Slater's partnership with Brown and Almy did not last. Slater's business strategy was to specialize in manufacturing thread and yarn; Brown and Almy wanted to incorporate the entire range of operations, from spinning yarn to weaving cloth. Because of their disagreement, Slater broke with his partners and built his own mill across the river in 1797. He rented rooms from Oziel Wilkinson (1744–1815), and later married his daughter Hannah. Wilkinson and two of his wife's brothers became new partners with Slater, and together they constructed the mill town of Slatersville, Rhode Island. In 1806, Slater's brother John (1776–1843) arrived from England, bringing with him a variety of tools not available in the United States (as well as seeds for garden plants not available in New England), and joined his brother's business. By 1807, Slatersville was the largest mill town in New England, but it was so compact that workers seldom had to travel more than a quarter mile to get from their factory housing to their jobs, the store, or church.

The father of the American Industrial Revolution

In his career, Slater was a partner in, or founder of, thirteen textile mills, making him one of the most successful businessmen in early American history. Not only did he help transfer English technology to the United States; he also developed business and management ideas that became important in the success of U.S. industry throughout the nineteenth century. His early desire to specialize in one aspect of the textile business, spinning thread, was paralleled by his development of specialization of work inside his mills.

Slater's life illustrated one of the most important contributions that he and other immigrants made to the growing United States: ideas. In the case of Slater, it was the idea of how to build an advanced factory to spin cotton into thread, as well as ideas about employing whole families in the mills. As a result, the United States eventually began to compete with (and eventually overtook) England in manufacturing using the techniques and equipment of the Industrial Revolution.

Although Slater may be celebrated as an American hero for introducing manufacturing technology to the United States just a decade after independence from Britain, he is regarded by some as a thief. England and the United States both had laws protecting inventors from having their ideas stolen, and there is little doubt that Slater reproduced the idea of Arkwright's spinning machines without paying anything. Had he reproduced equipment invented inside the United States, Slater could have been fined for violating a patent, an exclusive right to benefit from an idea for a designated period of time. But U.S. patent laws only protected inventions created in the United States; stealing an idea from Britain and bringing it across the ocean was considered fair game in the late eighteenth century.

Slater died in 1835 with an estate valued at over $1 million at the time (the equivalent of about $17 million in the twenty-first century).

—*James L. Outman*

For More Information

Books

Cameron, Edward H. *Samuel Slater, Father of the American Manufactures*. Freeport, ME: B. Wheelwright Co., 1960.

Loeb, Robert H. *New England Village: Everyday Life in 1810*. Garden City, NY: Doubleday, 1976.

Tucker, Barbara. *Samuel Slater and the Origins of the American Textile Industry, 1790–1860*. Ithaca, NY: Cornell University Press, 1984.

White, George. *Memoir of Samuel Slater, the Father of American Manufactures; Connected with the History of the Rise and Progress of the Cotton Manufacture in England and America*. New York: A. M. Kelley, 1967.

Periodicals

Gustaitis, Joseph. "Samuel Slater: Father of the Industrial Revolution." *American History Illustrated* (May 1989): p. 32.

"The Memory of Samuel Slater." *Yankee* (August 1999): p. 108.

Tucker, Barbara M. "The Merchant, the Manufacturer, and the Factory Manager: The Case of Samuel Slater." *Business History Review* (Autumn 1981): p. 297.

Web Sites

"Samuel Slater." *Samuel Slater: Father of the American Industrial Revolution.* http://www.woonsocket.org/slaterhist.htm (accessed on March 26, 2004).

"The Story of Samuel Slater." *Slater Mill: A Living History Museum.* http://www.slatermill.org/html/history.html (accessed on March 26, 2004).

Statue of Liberty

Built (work completed) in 1884
France

Unveiled in 1886
New York Harbor, New York

America's symbol of democracy and
welcome to immigrants

I n New York Harbor, the Statue of Liberty, an elegant lady holding a torch to light the way for hundreds of thousands of European immigrants, is a stirring symbol of both the United States and its welcoming embrace of "huddled masses yearning to breathe free." The image of the statue is widely reproduced as a celebration of the American political system and the country's history as a collection of immigrants who together built a new nation on the North American continent. Like written documents such as the Declaration of Independence (1776) declaring that "all men are created equal," the Statue of Liberty has a long history behind its symbolism.

The Statue of Liberty began as a joint vision in the eyes of two Frenchmen: sculptor Frédéric Auguste Bartholdi (1834–1904) and politician Éduoard-René Lefebvre de Laboulaye (1811–1883). They met at a dinner party in 1863 or 1865 (authors differ on the date), where Laboulaye sketched out an idea for a statue that would symbolize the role of the United States as a model for the freedom-loving republic, a government in which power lay in the hands of the people, instead of a king, Laboulaye wanted to see in France. At the time, France was gov-

"From her beacon-hand / Glows world-wide welcome ..."

Statue of Liberty. © *Kelly-Mooney Photography/Corbis.*

Frédéric Auguste Bartholdi, the French sculptor and designer of the Statue of Liberty. *Getty Images.*

erned by Louis-Napoléon Bonaparte (1808–1873), who had been given dictatorial, or authoritarian, powers in 1852 after a popular election. Laboulaye disliked this type of rule.He and Bartholdi had in mind for France to present as a gift to the United States an enormous statue that on the surface would symbolize the friendship of the two countries during the American War of Independence against Britain (1776–81), when France provided military aid to the American rebels. The deeper meaning of the statue for Laboulaye and Bartholdi would come from the symbolic torchlight that it would cast, showing the French people the way to claim their own liberty by reestablishing a republic in France. The concept of immigration had nothing to do with their plan.

Bartholdi plunged into the project enthusiastically. It would take him almost two decades to complete the statue. He made several trips to the United States to generate enthusiasm for the project, and to launch a drive to raise funds to build a base on which the statue could stand. In visits to New York, Bartholdi noticed a tiny island in New York harbor, just off the southern tip of Manhattan, called Bedloe's Island, that he thought would be the perfect place for the statue. Meanwhile in France, Bartholdi and Laboulaye set about raising funds to make the statue itself.

Years before the project was complete, Laboulaye's political dream was realized. In September 1870, after a disastrous war between France and Prussia (now part of Germany), the emperor, Bonaparte, was deposed by an act of Parliament, and a new republic, called the Third Republic, was declared. But the project for a Statue of Liberty was already advancing.

Building the statue

One of Bartholdi's inspirations for the new statue was the Colossus of Rhodes, which had been built in 282 B.C.E. on

The Statue of Liberty's head and crown.
© *Bettmann/Corbis.*

the Mediterranean island of Rhodes to commemorate the successful defense of the island against Greek invaders. That statue had stood at the harbor of the island, with one foot placed on either side of the water passage, so that ships could pass between the legs. The Colossus (the word means "gigantic") became one of the Wonders of the World, alongside the Egyptian pyramids—marvels of construction in ancient history. The Colossus of Rhodes did not last long, however. An earthquake in about 226 B.C.E. caused the statue's legs to buckle and it fell into a heap, eventually to be dismantled and sold as scrap metal hundreds of years later.

Inside Bartholdi's statue was a framework built by Gustav Eiffel (1832–1932), a French engineer who pioneered the construction of very tall structures using iron. Eiffel's most famous structure is the Eiffel Tower in Paris, which has served for over a century as an international symbol of Paris, much as the Statue of Liberty has served as a symbol of New York City.

Bartholdi molded three hundred copper sheets that covered the interior framework; the copper eventually turned into a greenish hue after long exposure to the atmosphere. The face of the statue was modeled after the face of the sculptor's own mother; the arms, one holding a torch and the other clutching a tablet, were modeled after the arms of Bartholdi's wife.

The symbolism of the Statue of Liberty

The Statue of Liberty was not simply a representation of a woman; it was intended from the very start as a political statement. Consequently, virtually every detail of the statue carried a message, starting with the fact that the statue represented a woman.

For many years before the Statue of Liberty was designed, female figures had been used to represent both countries and political ideas. In North America, Native American princess Pocahontas (c. 1595–1617), reputed to have saved English settler John Smith (1580–1631) from execution at the hands of her father, chief Powhatan (c. 1550–1618), had been used by artists to represent one characteristic of the United States: a new country where Europeans could find refuge, a country untouched by the corruption and history of Europe. In France, similarly, artist Eugene Delacroix (1798–1863) represented the French Revolution (1789) in his painting "Liberty Leading the People" as a woman carrying a rifle in one hand and the flag of France in the other leading a crowd into battle. (The French Revolution overthrew, and eventually executed, King Louis XVI [1754–1793; reigned 1774–93], and established a republic, a form of government in which power rests in the hands of the citizens rather than a monarch.) In the United States, just a few years before the Statue of Liberty project, the U.S. Congress in 1855 had commissioned a statue of a woman, called Lady Freedom, to stand on top of the dome of the U.S. Capitol. Lady Freedom was equipped with a sword and a helmet, representing the notion of a nation that was willing to fight for its democratic form of government.

Not all figures symbolizing the United States were women. The figure of Uncle Sam also was used in newspaper and magazine drawings to represent the United States. In the years before the Statue of Liberty was designed, representations of Uncle Sam found in newspaper cartoons had come to represent the physical figure of President Abraham Lincoln (1809–1865; served 1861–65). Uncle Sam was, generally, meant to represent ordinary Americans, voting citizens who were the basis of the country's political structure.

The Statue of Liberty was shown wearing a long, flowing robe, resembling the toga of ancient Greece and Rome. In the nineteenth century, the worlds of ancient Greece and Rome represented an idealistic time when the idea of a republic and democracy, or government by popular vote, were first conceived and implemented. Lady Liberty's gown was intended to evoke the ideals of that ancient era. Modern copies of ancient Greek and Roman statues had become popular throughout Europe in the eighteenth century as part of the movement called the Renaissance, or rebirth, of classical traditions in the fourteenth through sixteenth centuries. Renaissance thinkers examined classical traditions not only in art but also in politics, substituting some of the philosophical principles of ancient Greece and Rome for the religious ideals of the Bible.

In her left hand, the statue clutches a tablet, on which is inscribed "1776." The date refers to the year in which the U.S. Declaration of Independence was signed by the Continental Congress in Philadelphia, Pennsylvania, declaring that Britain's colonies in North America intended to become an independent nation, based on the belief that "all men are created equal" and that when governments fail to uphold mankind's natural rights to "life, liberty and the pursuit of happiness" citizens have a natural right to overthrow that government and establish a new one. The tablet in Lady Liberty's arms also has a larger, religious significance: It

The Statue of Liberty holds a torch that symbolizes the freedom found in the United States. © *Richard Berenholtz/Corbis.*

evokes the memory of the biblical story of Moses carrying God's ten commandments written on a tablet down from Mount Sinai.

In her other hand, Lady Liberty holds a torch, symbolizing the light that the United States holds up for the world—and especially France, in the opinion of Bartholdi—showing the ideal path to follow in politics. On her head, the statue wears a spiked crown, called a diadem, symbolizing the rays of the sun. The crown is a reference to the Colossus of Rhodes, which was intended in ancient times as a statue of Helios, the sun god. Finally, at her feet, lay broken shackles (metal bands to hold arms and legs with chains), representing the political repression of Europe from which the United States had broken free.

In 1871, Bartholdi wrote in a letter to Laboulaye: "I will try to glorify the Republic and Liberty over there, in the hope that someday I will find it again here [in France]."

Setting up the statue

Bartholdi finished work on the statue in France in 1884. The entire structure was then dismantled and packed into two hundred cases to be sent by ship to New York. There, however, loomed a potential problem: how to pay for the statue's base? The size of the statue meant that it needed a large, and very heavy, pedestal to anchor it to the ground. Bartholdi's project had not generated much interest in the United States, and the government was not willing to pay the cost of building the pedestal. Finally, a newspaper publisher, **Joseph Pulitzer** (1847–1911; see entry in volume 2), came to the rescue. Pulitzer, an immi-

grant from Hungary, published the *New York World,* a popular newspaper read by working people, and he used his newspaper to solicit public donations for building the pedestal. One hundred thousand contributors raised $120,000 in just five months to pay for the pedestal.

Part of the fund raising drive included an art auction in 1883, and a New York writer and poet, **Emma Lazarus** (1849–1887; see entry in volume 2), contributed a poem to the cause. It was titled "The New Colossus." Lazarus, who was Jewish, had become interested in the plight of Jews in Russia who were victims, in 1880 and 1881, of pogroms, or massacres of Jews that were permitted by the government of Russia. The attacks caused many Jews to wish to flee to a safer place. Lazarus herself advocated that Jews move to Palestine and reestablish the ancient state of Israel. In practice, however, large numbers of Jews from eastern Europe, along with other poor Europeans from Italy, Greece, and other countries of southern Europe, were immigrating to the United States. Lazarus was active in organizations set up to help Jewish immigrants adjust to their new land. Her poem was barely noticed.

Thanks to the popular fund-raising, money was found to build the pedestal, designed by prominent architect Richard Morris Hunt (1828–1895). When complete, the pedestal was 89 feet high. It included 24,000 tons of concrete, the largest mass of concrete made at the time.

Finally, on October 28, 1886, more than a million people turned out on a rainy, foggy day to watch a parade in Manhattan marking the unveiling of the statue. President Grover Cleveland (1837–1908; served 1885–89 and 1893–97) came to New York for the ceremony. In his speech, he spoke of freedom and democracy, but never mentioned immigration.

Six years after Lady Liberty was set up on Bedloe's Island, the U.S. government used another island in New York Harbor, Ellis Island, as the site of a new center for processing immigrants. There, within sight of the Statue of Liberty, millions of people first came ashore to undergo health checks before being admitted to the United States. The flood of immigrants passing through Ellis Island between its opening and 1924 (when a new U.S. immigration law severely restricted immigration) represented the largest single flow of immigrants in the country's history. The realization that many of the newcomers were poor, were not Protestants (many were Catholics, from southern Europe, and others were Jews), and had darker skin than earlier immigrants from Britain and northern Europe, was not pleasing to many. *Judge* magazine in 1890 published a cartoon in which the Statue of Liberty was depicted as cringing as two ships dumped loads of garbage onto her base—symbolizing the poor immigrants.

In 1895, American novelist and poet Thomas Bailey Aldrich (1836–1907) wrote a poem about immigrants titled

"Unguarded Gates," by Thomas Bailey Aldrich

Wide open and unguarded stand our gates,
Named of the four winds, North, South, East and West;
Portals that lead to an enchanted land
Of cities, forests, fields of living gold,
Vast prairies, lordly summits touched with snow,
Majestic rivers sweeping proudly past
The Arab's date-palm and the Norseman's pine—
A realm wherein are fruits of every zone,
Airs of all climes, for lo! throughout the year
The red rose blossoms somewhere—a rich land,
A later Eden planted in the wilds,
With not an inch of earth within its bound
But if a slave's foot press it sets him free.
Here, it is written, Toil shall have its wage,
And Honor honor, and the humblest man
Stand level with the highest in the law.
Of such a land have men in dungeons dreamed,
And with the vision brightening in their eyes
Gone smiling to the fagot and the sword.
Wide open and unguarded stand our gates,
And through them presses a wild motley throng—
Men from the Volga and the Tartar steppes,
Featureless figures of the Hoang-Ho,
Malayan, Scythian, Teuton, Kelt, and Slav,
Flying the Old World's poverty and scorn;
These bringing with them unknown gods and rites,
Those, tiger passions, here to stretch their claws.
In street and alley what strange tongues are loud,
Accents of menace alien to our air,
Voices that once the Tower of Babel knew!
O Liberty, white Goddess! Is it well
To leave the gates unguarded? On thy breast
Fold Sorrow's children, soothe the hurts of fate,
Lift the down-trodden, but with hand of steel
Stay those who to thy sacred portals come
To waste the gifts of freedom. Have a care
Lest from thy brow the clustered stars be torn
And trampled in the dust. For so of old
The thronging Goth and Vandal trampled Rome,
And where the temples of the Caesars stood
The lean wolf unmolested made her lair.

"The New Colossus" by Emma Lazarus

Not like the brazen giant of Greek fame,
With conquering limbs astride from land to land;
Here at our sea-washed, sunset gates shall stand
A mighty woman with a torch, whose flame
Is the imprisoned lightning, and her name
Mother of Exiles. From her beacon-hand
Glows world-wide welcome; her mild eyes command
The air-bridged harbor that twin cities frame.
"Keep ancient lands, your storied pomp!" cries she
With silent lips. "Give me your tired, your poor,
Your huddled masses yearning to breathe free,
The wretched refuse of your teeming shore.
Send these, the homeless, tempest-tost to me,
I lift my lamp beside the golden door!"

"Unguarded Gates." Aldrich appealed to the symbolic Statue of Liberty to be wary of immigrants, in case they should not honor America's commitment to freedom and instead destroy the country, much as invading barbarians had attacked the majesty of ancient Rome. For Aldrich, the Statue of Liberty was not a welcoming lamp for immigrants so much as a symbol of a country that might be changed for the worse by newcomers who were not white and might not share the values represented by the Statue of Liberty.

The Statue assumes her place as a symbol

Not until 1903 did a New York philanthropist, or a person who gives away money to benefit society, and friend of Emma Lazarus come across the nearly forgotten "The New Colossus" in a bookshop and arranged to have the last five lines of the poem engraved on a plaque and attached to the base of the statue. Only then did the Statue of Liberty take on her role as a symbol of both American political freedoms and America's welcoming arms extended to immigrants. The poem that Lazarus had contributed two decades earlier to help pay for the pedestal of the statue was reproduced on a plaque. Titled "The New Colossus," the poem turned the Statue of Liberty into something quite different from the conception of Aldrich in 1895. Instead of a symbol of an America about to be polluted by immigrants, Lazarus's poem turned the Statue of Liberty into a symbol of refuge and hope.

In the century since Lazarus's poem was placed on its base, the Statue of Liberty has come to symbolize the ideals of the United States, as it was originally intended to do by Bartholdi. It also serves as a beacon to refugees wishing to flee their homelands and come to the United States to be free of oppression and persecution, as well as to make a fortune.

As a symbol of the American form of government, however, the Statue of Liberty has always enjoyed an important place in American life. Images of the statue have been widely reproduced, and were everywhere during the 1976 celebrations marking two centuries of independence for the United States of America. The Statue of Liberty has also fulfilled its original mission far outside the United States. In 1989, for example, student demonstrators demanding more civil liberties in Beijing, the capital of China, created a replica of the Statue of Liberty to symbolize their protest. It was a moment that demonstrated how the power of an idea can transcend whatever differences may separate one people from another in space and time.

—*James L. Outman*

For More Information

Books

Aldrich, Thomas Bailey. *Unguarded and Other Poems*. Boston, New York: Houghton Mifflin and Company, 1895.

Allen, Leslie. *Liberty: The Statue and the American Dream*. New York: Statue of Liberty–Ellis Island Foundation with the cooperation of the National Geographic Society, 1985.

Holland, F. Ross. *Idealists, Scoundrels, and the Lady: An Insider's View of the Statue of Liberty–Ellis Island Project*. Urbana: University of Illinois Press, 1993.

Merriam, Eve. *Emma Lazarus, Woman with a Torch*. New York: Citadel Press, 1956.

Trachtenberg, Marvin. *The Statue of Liberty*. New York: Viking Press, 1976.

Periodicals

Dowling, Claudia Glenn. "The Landing of a Landmark; From French-man's Folly to American Icon." *Life* (July 1986): p. 50.

Galante, Pierre. "The Man Behind the Statue of Liberty" (Auguste Bartholdi). *Good Housekeeping* (July 1986): p. 101.

Web Sites

Fulford, James. "Immigration Myths (contd.): The Statue of Immigration, or *Liberty Inviting the World*." *VDARE.com.* http://www.vdare.com/fulford/statue_of_immigration.htm (accessed on March 26, 2004).

Liberty State Park: The Statue of Liberty and Ellis Island. http://www.libertystatepark.com (accessed on March 26, 2004).

Smith, John. "Letter to Queen Anne Regarding Pocahontas." *Mayflower-History.com.* http://members.aol.com/mayflo1620/pocahontas.html (accessed on March 26, 2004).

"Statue of Liberty National Monument." *National Park Service.* http://www.nps.gov/stli/ (accessed on March 26, 2004).

Danny Thomas

Born January 6, 1914
Deerfield, Michigan

Died February 6, 1991
Los Angeles, California

Television star and producer; founder, St. Jude's Children's Research Hospital

Danny Thomas was a television star of the 1950s and 1960s and a producer of such hit television series as *The Andy Griffith Show, The Dick Van Dyke Show, Gomer Pyle,* and *The Mod Squad.* His success in television allowed him to keep a vow he made in prayer in 1940, when he was struggling to support his family. Learning that St. Jude was the patron saint of hopeless causes, Thomas prayed to the saint, asking for direction. In return for the saint's help, Thomas vowed to build a shrine for St. Jude. Soon afterward, he had his big break as a performer at a nightclub in Chicago, Illinois. He won a regular contract and went on to become a major star on radio and television. In 1962, after funding the construction he dedicated the St. Jude's Children's Research Hospital, in Memphis, Tennessee, a leader in the fight against childhood diseases. As Thomas noted, it was his greatest accomplishment and contribution during his lifetime.

"That's my epitaph. It's right on the cornerstone [of St. Jude's Children's Research Hospital]: Danny Thomas, founder."

Family storytelling

Born Muzyad Yakhoob on January 6, 1914, in a farmhouse in Deerfield, Michigan, Thomas was the fifth of nine

Danny Thomas. *Getty Images.*

children of Charles and Margaret Christen Jacobs, Catholic immigrants from Lebanon. His parents Americanized the family name from Yakhoob to Jacobs, and Thomas's first name was Americanized from Muzyad to Amos. He grew up as Amos Jacobs in various locations between southeastern Michigan and northern Ohio. From his family and relatives who visited, he learned the art of storytelling. Later, as a comedy entertainer, he was known for his funny stories, rather than for jokes. "My people are inherently storytellers," Thomas told Mervyn Rothstein of the *New York Times*. "When I was a kid, the entertainment was somebody from the old country or a big city who came and visited and told tales of where they came from."

Thomas began performing as a teenager with one of his brothers, Ray, in an act called "Songs, Dances, and Happy Patter." He quit school at age sixteen to become a professional entertainer, but his first professional experience was selling candy at a burlesque, or comedy, theater in Toledo, Ohio. At age twenty, he began singing on a radio station in Detroit, Michigan. Two years later, on January 15, 1936, he married Rose Marie Cassaniti. They would have three children, Margaret Julia (Marlo), Theresa Cecelia (Terre), and Charles Anthony (Tony), all of whom were to be successful in show business. Marlo and Terre Thomas became actresses (Marlo had a hit comedy television series in the 1960s called *That Girl*), and Tony Thomas became a television producer.

Between his radio job and nightclub performances, however, Thomas was barely able to make a living. In nightclubs, he began performing under the name Danny Thomas because he had succeeded in radio and was embarrassed to still be playing small nightclubs to help make ends meet. He was playing in clubs in Chicago in 1940 to help support his wife, who was back in Detroit and pregnant with their first child, when he learned that St. Jude was the patron saint of hopeless causes. Thomas prayed to the saint, asking for direction. In return, he promised to build a shrine for St. Jude.

Soon after that prayer, Thomas earned his big break in show business at the 5100 Club in Chicago, where his stories and folksy songs were a hit with audiences. He signed a two-year contract to perform at the club and moved his family to Chicago. "My real birthday is August 12, 1940," Thomas later told Howard Reich of the *Chicago Tribune*. That was the day, he noted, "when I opened at the 5100 Club, and I've been celebrating it every year since." Reich noted that with the contract at the 5100 Club, Thomas had "graduated from working rowdy weddings, washing-machine conventions, two-bit burlesque houses and small-time radio programs (where he created the sounds of the hooves of the Lone Ranger's horse) … and a star was born."

National star

Thomas's popularity steadily increased during the 1940s. He became host of *The Danny Thomas Show* on national radio from 1944 to 1949. He entertained American troops during World War II (1939–45) in Europe and Asia. After the war, Thomas appeared in his first film, *The Unfinished Dance* (1947). He later played popular music composer Gus Kahn (1886–1941) in the film *I'll See You in My Dreams* (1951) and starred in a remake of *The Jazz Singer* (1953).

During the 1950s, two circumstances would lead to Thomas's most enduring role as an entertainer. Television was becoming more prominent, entering what is called its "Golden Age," when television replaced radio and movies as the most popular medium for news and entertainment. During 1951 and 1952, Thomas had been one of four rotating hosts for *All-Star Revue,* a television variety show, but he left to return to performing in nightclubs.

Thomas began discussing television situation-comedy ("sit-com") concepts with writer Mel Shavelson (1917–). In addition, the Thomas family had moved to Los Angeles. Thomas wanted to be with his family more often than he was able to as a touring entertainer and movie actor. As he recalled in his 1991 autobiography, *Make Room for Danny,* "I was away on the road so much that they hardly knew me. They called me 'Uncle Daddy.'" He made that remark to Shavelson, who turned it into the premise of a comedy show: it would be about a nightclub entertainer trying to have a normal family life along with a career in show business. Thomas's wife Rose Marie suggested the show should be titled *Make Room for Daddy.* She explained that while Thomas was on tour, the children played in his area of the home. When he returned, they had to move their playthings back to their bedroom to "make room for Daddy."

Make Room for Daddy made its debut on ABC television in September 1953. Despite winning Emmy Awards (television's highest award) for Best Situation Comedy Series and Best Actor in a Regular Series, the show had poor viewer ratings for four seasons. The show moved to CBS in 1957, was renamed *The Danny Thomas Show,* and introduced some new characters. Also Thomas's on-screen wife, Jean Hagen (1923–1977), left the show. The character became the first one to "die" in an ongoing television series. The next season of the series started with Thomas's on-screen children being told, "Mommy's gone to Heaven." Thomas's character then remarried, took on a precocious five year-old stepdaughter, and was visited regularly by a Lebanese relative, Uncle Tonoose. The new series was a hit and remained so through the end of its run in 1964.

By that time, Thomas had also become a television producer of two popular situation comedies, *The Andy Griffith Show* and *The Dick Van Dyke Show.* He made a shrewd investment in the new Sands Hotel in Las Vegas, just before that city became an entertainment and gambling center.

He made enough money to pay back the promise he had made in a prayer in 1940, when he was struggling. In 1962, he dedicated St. Jude's Children's Research Hospital, in Memphis, Tennessee, to fight against childhood diseases. "That's my epitaph. It's right on the cornerstone: Danny Thomas, founder," Thomas told an interviewer in the *New York Times*. Shortly before his death, Thomas told the *Chicago Tribune,* "When I first prayed to St. Jude on that dark day in the Great Depression when my wife was expecting our first child, Marlo, I asked him to show me my way in life and I vowed to build him a shrine."

Although he later starred in the longest-running situation comedy in television history up to that time and became one of TV's top producers, Danny Thomas once called television a "workplace for idiots." He had spent two years as a rotating host with comedians Jack Carson (1910–1963), Jimmy Durante (1893–1980), and Ed Wynn (1886–1966) on an NBC variety show called *All-Star Revue*. He quit the show in 1952 to return to the nightclub circuit. A year later, he was back on television and becoming one of the leading stars of television's "Golden Age."

Granddaddy and fund-raiser

Make Room for Daddy and *The Danny Thomas Show* became the longest-running situation comedy in television history up to that time. It was still popular when it came to its end in 1964. That popularity inspired a reunion television special, *Make More Room for Daddy,* in 1967 on NBC—marking the third network to broadcast the same situation comedy. Two years later, another special aired, *Make Room for Granddaddy,* with most of the same cast; that special led to a regular series on ABC that ran during the 1970–71 season. In 1976–77, Thomas starred as Dr. Jules Bedford in the NBC-TV comedy *The Practice*.

Meanwhile, Thomas's daughter Marlo had a hit situation comedy on ABC with her show, *That Girl*. Thomas's son Tony would later be a successful producer of television comedy series, including *The Golden Girls* and *Empty Nest*. In 1991,

Danny Thomas (far right) with his daughter, Marlo, and her husband, talk show host Phil Donahue in July 1980. © *Bettmann/Corbis.*

Danny Thomas made a rare guest appearance on his son's show, *Empty Nest.* A week after the episode aired, he died of a heart attack.

Thomas had devoted much of his time during the 1970s and 1980s to raising money for his favorite charity, St. Jude's Hospital. For his tireless efforts on behalf of medical research, he was nominated for the Nobel Peace Prize in 1980 and 1981 and was awarded the Congressional Medal of Honor in 1985.

Thomas's memoir, *Make Room for Danny,* was published in 1991. In his popular storytelling style, Thomas recounted life from his birth on a farm—his mother was attended to during the birth by a local veterinarian—and his struggles and successes. Thomas was inducted into the Academy of Television Arts and Sciences Hall of Fame in 1991.

—*Roger Matuz*

For More Information

Books

McNeil, Alex. *Total Television: A Comprehensive Guide to Programming from 1948 to the Present.* New York: Penguin, 1991.

Sackett, Susan. *Prime-Time Hits: Television's Most Popular Network Programs.* New York: Billboard, 1993.

Thomas, Danny, and Bill Davidson. *Make Room for Danny.* New York: Putnam, 1991.

Periodicals

Reich, Howard. "A Nose for Show Biz. On His 77th Birthday, Danny Thomas Says He's Hardly the Retiring Type." *Chicago Tribune* (January 6, 1991): p. 10.

Rothstein, Mervyn. "Danny Thomas Puts His Life and Work on Paper." *New York Times* (January 10, 1991): p. C22.

Rothstein, Mervyn. "Danny Thomas, 77, the TV Star of 'Make Room for Daddy,' Dies." *New York Times* (February 7, 1991): p. D25.

Web Sites

The Danny Thomas Show aka Make Room for Daddy Website. http://www.timvp.com/dannyt.html (accessed on March 26, 2004).

"Danny's Promise." *St. Jude Children's Research Hospital.* http://www.stjude.org/about-st-jude/0,2569,460_3202_5798,00.html (accessed on March 26, 2004).

Alexis de Tocqueville

Born July 19, 1805
Paris, France

Died April 16, 1859
Cannes, France

French writer who first defined the meaning of American as a new nationality

> "[Americans] seem to me stinking with national conceit; it pierces through all their courtesy."

Alexis de Tocqueville.
AP/World Wide Photos.

Alexis de Tocqueville was a French aristocrat, or member of the upper class, sent to the United States in 1831 to study American prisons. He kept a detailed diary of his nine-month visit, and later wrote a book, *Democracy in America*. Tocqueville's journals and book described the ordinary, day-to-day aspects of American society. He thought that democracy could explain the many differences between the habits of Americans and the habits of Europeans, but it might be just as accurate to say that American society reflected the differences that emerged as a result of emigration. His writing addressed the issue of just what it meant to emigrate from a European society to another society in North America.

A young aristocrat in France

Alexis Charles Henri Maurice Clèrel de Tocqueville was the son of an aristocratic family from Normandy, in northern France. He was born at a time in French history when the aristocracy was threatened with extinction. Tocqueville was born in 1805, sixteen years after the French revolution of 1789. During the revolution, a large number of aristocrats (including one of Tocqueville's grandfathers) and the king of France, Louis XVI (1754–1793, reigned 1774–93), were executed by mobs intent on establishing a new republic in France. When Tocqueville was born, Louis-Napoléon Bonaparte (1769–1821) was emperor of France, trying to extend French influence over much of Europe. Most European countries were still ruled by established monarchies, or governments headed by a king or a queen.

The French background of Tocqueville's studies

France was often in turmoil during Tocqueville's early years. While Tocqueville was a boy, Napoléon ruled France as the emperor and the country was at war as Napoléon tried to extend France's control to most of Europe. The French army was defeated and Napoléon was sent into exile just as Tocqueville was coming into his teens. The royal family, forced out in 1789, was temporarily restored to power. During the 1820s, France was engaged in what was called the "Great Debate" over whether it was better to have a republic, in which the head of state is elected democratically, or to have a king. In 1830, another revolution took place that replaced one king with another. The new monarch's powers were limited by the popularly elected parliament, or legislature.

This background of French politics played an important role in Tocqueville's tour of the United States in 1831 and 1832, when he was observing what kind of differences in society might come about as a result of a democracy. For Tocqueville, the question related to what might happen in France if a government similar to that of the United States were established.

Tocqueville was educated privately as a boy. He then studied law in Paris from 1823 to 1826, after which he was appointed as an unpaid magistrate, or judge, in Versailles, near Paris.

On tour in America

In 1830, Tocqueville was asked to go to the United States along with his close friend Gustave de Beaumont (1802–1866) to conduct a study of the country's prison system.

Their tour lasted nine months, from May 1831 to February 1832. In this time, Tocqueville and Beaumont traveled from Newport, Rhode Island, as far south as New Orleans, Louisiana, and as far north as the British province of Quebec, in Canada.

The two young Frenchmen—Tocqueville was just twenty-six when he started his tour and Beaumont was twenty-nine—met dozens of local officials, ranging from U.S. president Andrew Jackson (1767–1845; served 1829–37) and former president John Quincy Adams (1767–1848; served 1825–29) to local mayors and judges. Often treated as celebrities, the two generally stayed in boardinghouses, or private homes whose owners rented out rooms to travelers, and met many ordinary Americans. Both men kept extensive diaries, although only Tocqueville's has survived, and wrote letters to family and friends in France.

Tocqueville and Beaumont jointly prepared an extensive report on American prisons, the official reason for their visit, as well as books about their trip. Of all their writings, Tocqueville's book *Democracy in America,* first published in 1835 with a second volume in 1840, was by far the best known. The book was a best-seller when it was published and has remained the subject of interest, especially in the United States, ever since. *Democracy in America* remains a unique study of everyday American society during a period of rapid growth made possible by a steady immigration of Europeans to the United States.

Tocqueville's work focused on the United States as an established society. In fact, however, a large portion of the population in 1831 had been born outside the United States and emigrated from their native lands. The population of the United States had grown from about seven million in 1810 to almost thirteen million in 1830, an increase of nearly 82 percent. (In the next two decades, from 1830 to 1850, the population would grow by 80 percent again.) A significant portion of the increase before 1830 reflected emigration from Britain; after 1830, German and Irish immigrants contributed heavily to population growth.

The American character

In New York, a few weeks into the start of his tour, Tocqueville wrote a letter to a former teacher in France, in

"My Dear Mother..."

In addition to *Democracy in America,* in which he recorded his observations of American society, Tocqueville also wrote many letters to his family and friends in France. This correspondence provided an insight into the practical details of his tour. In one letter to his mother, written from New York State, he wrote:

> You no doubt want to know, my dear mother, what is our present manner of life. It is this: We get up at five or six and we work till eight. At eight o'clock the bell announces breakfast. Every one goes in promptly. After that we go out to visit a few establishments or to get into touch with certain men who are interesting to listen to. We return to dine at three o'clock. At five we usually go home to put our notes in order till seven, the hour at which we go out into society to take tea. This style of life is very agreeable and, I believe, very healthy.

> But it upsets all our settled habits. For instance, we were utterly astounded the first day to see the women come to breakfast at eight o'clock in the morning carefully dressed for the whole day. It's the same, we are told, in all the private houses. One can with great propriety call on a lady at nine o'clock in the morning.

> The absence of wine at our meals at first struck us as very disagreeable; and we still can't understand the multitude of things that they succeed in introducing into their stomachs here. You see, in addition to breakfast, dinner, and tea with which the Americans eat ham, they also eat a very copious supper.... That up to now is the only indisputable superiority that I grant them over us. But they see in themselves many others. These people seem to me stinking with national conceit; it pierces through all their courtesy.

which he noted the differences between Americans and Europeans. "I couldn't keep from laughing in my beard [to myself] on thinking of the difference 1,500 leagues [about 4,500 miles] of sea make in the position of men. I thought of the more than subordinate role that I played in France two months ago and of the comparatively elevated situation in which we were finding ourselves here, the little noise that our mission has made at home and that which it makes here, all because of this little bit of sea-water [the Atlantic Ocean] I just spoke of."

Tocqueville was writing about how his personal status had changed from a lowly assistant judge in France to a celebrity in New York. It was a measure, also, of how traveling across the Atlantic had more of an effect than a comparable journey by land within Europe: A person's social status also changed. As Tocqueville observed many times, American society, largely comprising immigrants or the sons and grandsons of immigrants, had become something different and unique. Immigrants had brought some of their habits and languages but left many social attitudes behind.

Tocqueville's observations covered a wide range of subjects, ranging from attitudes toward religion to table manners, attitudes toward public officials, and the poor treatment of Native Americans and African American slaves in the South, which he described as resulting in "such unparalleled atrocities as suffice to show that the laws of humanity have been totally perverted." In July 1831, near the start of his tour, Tocqueville encountered Native Americans for the first time in New York. The ones that he saw were "more or less drunk," he wrote, and one man in particular seemed close to death. "In the midst of this American society, so well policed, so sententious [moralistic], so charitable," he wrote in his journal, "a cold selfishness and complete insensibility prevails when it is a question of the natives of the country. The Americans of the United States do not let their dogs hunt the Indians as do the Spaniards in Mexico, but at bottom it is the same pitiless feeling which here, as everywhere else, animates [characterizes] the European race. This world here belongs to us, they tell themselves every day: the Indian race is destined for final destruction which one cannot prevent and which it is not desirable to delay. Heaven has not made them to become civilized; it is necessary that they die. Besides I do not want to get mixed up in it. I will not do anything against them: I will limit myself to providing everything that will hasten their ruin. In time I will have their lands and will be innocent of their death."

Emigration and the emergence of democracy

In his introduction to *Democracy in America*, Tocqueville wrote: "The emigrants who colonized the shores of America in the beginning of the seventeenth century somehow separated the democratic principle from all the principles that it had to contend with in the old communities of Europe, and transplanted it alone to the New World. It has there been able to spread in perfect freedom and peaceably to determine the character of the laws by influencing the manners of the country."

In most respects, Tocqueville admired what he saw of American society. Americans, he found, were highly moralistic without the benefit of government-recognized religions. They were intensely interested in earning money. Compared with European society, the United States enjoyed a high degree of equality among its citizens. Tocqueville explained much of this American character by pointing to the earliest English immigrants who settled in New England.

These men and women, he observed, "on leaving the mother country [England] … had, in general, no notion of superiority one over another. The happy and the powerful do not go into exile, and there are no surer guarantees of equality among men than poverty and misfortune." This shared attitude was an important element in creating the type of society Tocqueville observed: a dedication to equality that was generally not present in Europe.

Tocqueville thought that the social class of the early settlers in New England had made a major difference in the nature of American society. The immigrants who settled in New England "all belonged to the more independent classes of their native country [England] …, containing neither lords nor common people…. All, perhaps without a single exception, had received a good education, and many of them were known in Europe for their talents and their acquirements. The other colonies [in the South] had been founded by adventurers without families; the immigrants of New England brought with them the best elements of order and morality; they landed on the desert coast accompanied by their wives and children…. Nor did they cross the Atlantic to improve their situation or to increase their wealth; it was a purely intellectual craving [for religious freedom] that called them from the comforts of their former homes; and in facing the inevitable sufferings of exile their object was the triumph of an idea."

The character of the New England immigrants, Tocqueville thought, was transferred to most of the northern colonies and gave the United States its distinctive culture. In his work, Tocqueville attributed this American character to democracy, the notion that all citizens were created equal and had an equal voice in government. This system was in sharp contrast to Tocqueville's European experience, in which government power was concentrated in the head of state, usually a king or a queen, and in the hands of aristocrats, people who inherited large estates and influence over the government. In the France of Tocqueville's time, ordinary citizens had little influence on government.

Back to France

Tocqueville and Beaumont returned to France in early 1832 and never returned to the United States. Apart from his writings, Tocqueville married an English woman, Mary Mottley, in 1835 and the next year inherited a castle in Normandy. He also inherited the aristocratic title Compte de Tocqueville, but did not use it.

Tocqueville was elected to the French parliament in 1839 and was briefly the foreign minister a decade later. He soon retired from political life, however, and retired to his estate in Cannes, in southern France, where he died in 1859.

—*James L. Outman*

For More Information

Books

Mancini, Matthew J. *Alexis de Tocqueville*. New York: Twayne Publishers, 1994.

Reeves, Richard. *American Journey: Traveling with Tocqueville in Search of Democracy in America*. New York: Simon & Schuster, 1982.

Tocqueville, Alexis de. *Democracy in America*. New York: G. Dearborn & Co., 1838. Multiple reprints.

Tocqueville, Alexis de. *Selected Letters on Politics and Society*. Berkeley: University of California Press, 1985.

Periodicals

Dilday, K. A. "Tocqueville Saw It Coming." *The New York Times* (November 26, 2000): p. WK2.

Kimball, Roger. "Tocqueville Today." *New Criterion* (November 2000): p. 4.

Samuelson, Robert J. "Democracy in America: It Succeeds Because Politics Is Just One of Many Outlets for Its Passions and Ambitions." *Newsweek* (Novmber 13, 2000): p. 61.

Web Sites

The Alexis de Tocqueville Tour Exploring Democracy in America. http://www.tocqueville.org (accessed on March 26, 2004).

Tocqueville, Alexis de. *Democracy in America*. Online version at *American Studies at the University of Virginia*. http://xroads.virginia.edu/~HYPER/DETOC/toc_indx.html (accessed on March 26, 2004).

Harriet Tubman

Born c. 1820
Dorchester County, Maryland

Died March 10, 1913
Auburn, New York

African American abolitionist who helped slaves emigrate from the United States to freedom in Canada using the Underground Railroad

"I was a stranger in a strange land."

For millions of people from Europe, and later Asia, the United States was a beacon of freedom and opportunity. For millions of African Americans living in the United States from 1619 to 1863, however, the United States was a prison, a place of enslavement from which the only escape in the middle of the nineteenth century was Canada. Harriet Tubman was the most prominent African American who helped slaves make the dangerous journey to freedom on the Underground Railroad.

Tubman made an estimated twenty round trips from the North to the South, and back north to Canada during the 1850s, a time when escaping slaves were subject to arrest and forced return to bondage, even in the nonslave states of the North. For several years, Tubman, herself an escaped slave, lived in Canada where she could be safe from arrest. A large reward was offered in the South for her capture, but she later boasted: "I never ran my train off the track, and I never lost a passenger."

Life in bondage

Harriet Tubman was the daughter of slaves, Harriet and Benjamin Ross. Her name at birth was Araminta, but she

Harriet Tubman. *Granger Collection.*

later adopted her mother's name. Unlike her ten siblings, Harriet was not sold off, and remained with her parents into her adulthood. (Later, her parents were among the first slaves Harriet brought North.)

By most accounts, Harriet did not adapt well to the life of a slave. She preferred working outside to being a house slave, and was often rebellious. As a teenager, Harriet was accidentally involved in an incident involving a slave who had stopped working early. As his overseer was about to whip him, the slave ran away and the overseer threw a two-pound weight at him. The weight accidentally hit Harriet in the head; from then on, she was subject to seizures, events involving involuntary brain activity that often result in brief unconsciousness. "I grew up like a neglected weed," she once told an interviewer. In 1844, she married John Tubman.

Living in Maryland, Tubman was not far from Pennsylvania, which did not allow slavery. Tubman realized that her journey from Maryland to freedom in Pennsylvania was relatively short. (She had once consulted a lawyer to see whether the death of her mother's white master might entitle her and her mother to freedom under the law. The lawyer told her that she would have had a good case at the time, but that too much time had passed since the former owner's death to expect a court to grant her freedom.) In 1849, when she learned that her master was considering selling her, she made the move. She made her way alone to Philadelphia, where she found a job as a cook. She was free but lonely for her family. She resolved to return to Maryland and bring her relatives back with her to Pennsylvania, the start of her long career sparking a migration to freedom.

In one important respect, Harriet Tubman's story was unusual in the middle of the nineteenth century. For Tubman, freedom and opportunity meant leaving the United States, even as millions of Europeans were arriving in search of new freedom of opportunity in the land where, according to the U.S. Declaration of Independence, "all men are created equal."

The national debate over slavery

In the decade of the 1850s, a long national debate over slavery gathered speed in the United States. Many people in the

North had actively opposed slavery since the late eighteenth century, and abolitionists, people who thought the federal government should ban slavery everywhere in the country, had been active for decades. During the 1850s, several events occurred that heightened the debate and had a major impact on Tubman's career as a "Moses," as she was called for leading her people to freedom. (In the Bible, Moses is the man who led the enslaved Jewish people out of Egypt to freedom in Israel.)

As part of the national debate over whether to allow slavery in newly populated western territories, the U.S. Congress in 1850 passed the Fugitive Slave Act. This law meant that escaped slaves would not be free when they reached a northern state, such as Pennsylvania, that did not recognize slavery. For escaped slaves like Harriet Tubman, the law meant that they could not find freedom anywhere in the United States unless their owners acted to set them free.

In 1856, the U.S. Supreme Court ruled that a slave who had been taken to the free state of Illinois, and then back to the slave state of Missouri, was not entitled to freedom based on living in Illinois. In the famous *Dred Scott* decision, the Supreme Court went further and ruled that slaves were not entitled to human rights; under the law, they were property and could do nothing to free themselves.

These two legal developments, coming at a time when increasing numbers of people in the North felt that slavery violated the basic principles of the Declaration of Independence ("We believe these truths to be self-evident, that all men are created equal...."), created an exodus of people out of the United States in search of their freedom. Slavery had been abolished in the British Empire, which included Canada, in 1833, making Canada the destination of escaping slaves from the southern states. People who actively opposed slavery helped people escape by forming what was known as the Underground Railroad, a secret network of houses where escaping slaves could safely be hidden on their way to Canada.

Conductor on the Underground Railroad

The Fugitive Slave Act directly affected Harriet Tubman, who was in danger of being seized and sent back to Maryland as a slave. For six years, from 1851 to 1857, her

Harriet Tubman with a
group of slaves she helped.
Library of Congress.

main residence was in St. Catherines, Ontario. From there, she reentered the United States to help liberate slaves in the American South.

After her own lonely escape, Tubman became the most renowned "conductor" on the Underground Railroad. On an average of twice a year during the 1850s, Tubman traveled into the slave states, where she was widely known and where a reward was offered for her capture, to guide slaves northward to Canada. It was a dangerous task. Slave owners were highly aware that their slaves might run off, and groups of black people on the move created suspicions. Tubman became famous for outwitting slave owners. On at least one occasion, she bought railroad tickets heading south, further into slave territory, to make her party of escaping slaves seem like innocent travelers.

Using money she earned as a cook and laundry worker in Philadelphia, Tubman staged her first rescue within a year, traveling to Baltimore to meet her sister and two of her children and guide them to freedom in the North. Eventually, by 1857, she guided her entire family north.

Tubman began her crusade alone but later came into contact with leaders of the growing antislavery movement in the North. What started as a personal mission to rescue her family expanded to include many other slaves who wanted to immigrate to freedom. Tubman was short (just five feet tall) and hardly looked like a Moses of her people. She often disguised herself as an old woman to avoid being captured in the South. Whatever she lacked in physical stature, she more than made up in mental fortitude.

Tubman often carried a rifle, and she sometimes threatened the escaping slaves she was with if it seemed they were about to endanger the whole group. Like most slaves, Tubman was never taught to read and write; she had to rely on her memory. She used a complex code in communicating with the people she was leading to freedom, one based on biblical stories and slave songs. Her code also served as a measure to protect her "passengers" from capture. Her methods were effective: in a decade of leading slaves to freedom, she later boasted, she never lost a single one to professional slave hunters. Altogether, she led over three hundred slaves to freedom.

Eventually the governor of New York, William Seward (1801–1872), sold Tubman a house in Auburn, New York. Auburn is not far from Seneca Falls, New York, the site of the meeting that produced the first declaration of women's rights from the new and growing movement for female equality. Seward, who eventually became secretary of state during the administrations of Abraham Lincoln (1809–1865; served 1861–65) and Andrew Johnson (1808–1875; served 1865–69), was a strong supporter of Tubman and her work on the Underground Railroad.

Civil War and emancipation

The outbreak of the Civil War (1861–65) in April 1861 changed the character of Tubman's work, but not her goal. The war did not break out over the issue of slavery; it broke out over the issue of preserving the union of states that had come together to form the United States. President Lincoln himself declared that if he had been able to preserve the union half slave and half free, he would have done so. Nevertheless, victory for the North over the South—the Confederate States of America—seemed vital to the cause of freeing African Americans from bondage.

Consequently, Tubman started a second career as a spy for the North, a career for which her decade of risky travels in the South had prepared her. She also served as a nurse in conquered areas of the South.

As a spy, Tubman organized African American men to help the Union army scout ahead in South Carolina in preparation for Union attacks. On at least one occasion, she personally accompanied an army unit in South Carolina and came under fire, a highly unusual activity for a woman in the nineteenth century. In another role, Tubman helped care for newly freed slaves, teaching some of the basic survival skills they would need as free men and women.

After the war

After the Civil War, Tubman returned to her home in Auburn, New York. Despite her direct aid to the Union army as a spy, and her fame as a liberator of about three hundred slaves, Tubman was never rewarded in her lifetime. Her application to the government for the benefits enjoyed by other fighters for the Union cause was denied.

Nevertheless, she devoted her life to helping her fellow African Americans, caring for her aged parents, and raising funds for schools dedicated to former slaves. In 1896, she was able to buy land near her house, where in 1908 she opened the Harriet Tubman Home for Aged and Indigent Colored People. Two years later, Tubman herself moved into the home, where she lived for three years until she died of pneumonia on March 10, 1913.

—*James L. Outman*

For More Information

Books

Bentley, Judith. *Harriet Tubman*. New York: Franklin Watts, 1990.

Bradford, Sarah H. *Harriet: The Moses of Her People*. New York: G. R. Lockwood & Son, 1886. Multiple reprints.

Carlson, Judy. *Harriet Tubman: Call to Freedom*. New York: Fawcett Columbine, 1989.

Conrad, Earl. *Harriet Tubman*. New York: Eriksson, 1969.

Ruchames, Louis, ed. *The Abolitionists; a Collection of Their Writing*. New York: Putnam, 1963.

Periodicals

Bennett, Lerone Jr. "Free for Christmas: Harriet Tubman Leads Slave Escape and Gives the Greatest Gift of the Holiday Season." *Ebony* (December 1966): p. 80.

Donnelly, Matt. "Black Moses." *Christian History* (May 1999): p. 24.

Winkler, Peter. "Eyewitness on the Underground Railroad: History Owes a Lot to William Still." *National Geographic Explorer* (January-February 2002): p. 13.

Web Sites

"Aboard the Underground Railroad." *National Park Service*. http://www.cr.nps.gov/nr/travel/underground (accessed on March 26, 2004).

"National Underground Railroad Freedom Center." http://www.undergroundrailroad.org (accessed on March 26, 2004).

"The Underground Railroad." *National Geographic*. http://www.nationalgeographic.com/features/99/railroad (accessed on March 26, 2004).

An Wang

Born February 20, 1920
Shanghai, China

Died March 24, 1990
Boston, Massachusetts

Pioneer of computer-related innovations

"Progress does not follow a straight line; the future is not a mere projection of trends in the present. Rather, it is revolutionary. It overturns the conventional wisdom of the present, which often conceals or ignores the clues to the future."

An Wang. *AP/Wide World Photos.*

A visionary inventor and industrialist, Dr. An Wang was a pioneer of the computer age. From devising magnetic-memory cores in the 1940s that greatly increased the amount of data that could be stored in a computer and making the data easier and faster to retrieve, to introducing desktop word processors in the 1970s, Wang was a leading contributor in the evolution of computers from room-sized to desktop systems. He founded Wang Laboratories in Boston, Massachusetts, which became the largest minority-owned business in the United States and made him a billionaire. He was estimated to be the fifth richest man in America by *Forbes* magazine in 1984. Wang gave generously from this wealth to improve hospitals and neighborhoods, university programs and art centers. During the 1980s, Massachusetts governor (and 1988 presidential candidate) Michael Dukakis (1933–) said of Wang, "I don't know how many countless thousands and thousands of people owe a debt of gratitude for what he did."

Excelling amid turmoil

An Wang (his name can be translated as "Peaceful King") was born on February 20, 1920, in Shanghai, China. He was the oldest boy and second oldest child among the five children of Yin Lu and Zen Wan Chien. His father, an English teacher at a private elementary school 30 miles outside of Shanghai, was a strict disciplinarian and emphasized education. Wang attended the school where his father taught and proved an excellent student. He entered the equivalent of third grade when he was only six years old and was particularly strong in mathematics. At age seven, he began studying the English language. He scored highest in his class on a competitive exam to enter Shanghai Provincial High School, one of the best in China. He was thirteen years old when he entered high school, and sixteen when he entered the Chiao Tung University, a highly respected engineering school.

Wang and Ancestry

Until the time he was twenty-one, An Wang lived in either Shanghai or Kun San, where his father's ancestors had lived for six hundred years. Traditionally, some Chinese families keep a written family history that is updated every few generations. The Wang family had such a book that claimed to cover twenty-three generations, back to the time when Marco Polo journeyed from Europe to China. Writing about these books in *Lessons* (1986), his autobiography, Wang noted that such histories "gave our families a sense of continuity and permanence that I don't see in the more mobile West."

Meanwhile, China was in the midst of turmoil—in an era sometimes called the "Age of Confusion." Japan had invaded and occupied the Chinese province of Manchuria in 1931. There was civil strife among warlords, or regional leaders who ruled by force, within China. By 1939, when Wang was nineteen, World War II (1939–45) was underway and Japan was expanding its power in Asia. Wang was safe at the university, which was located inside a French-held district of Shanghai. He studied electrical engineering and communications. Wang graduated in 1940 and then worked as a teaching assistant.

In 1941, Wang volunteered with eight of his classmates for a secret mission. They went into a Japanese-occupied region to design and build transmitters and radios for Nationalist (Chinese) troops. He also worked at the Central Radio Works in Kweillin. The area was regularly shelled by Japanese artillery during the time Wang was there. In early 1945, he took advantage of a government-sponsored program that sent engineers to study in the United States, which had been a Chinese ally in World War II.

Wang was able to enroll in September 1945 at Harvard University, just as World War II was officially ending.

Wang excelled at Harvard, earning a master of science degree in 1946 and his doctor of philosophy (Ph.D.) degree in applied physics in 1948. That year, he met Lorraine Chiu at a function organized for Chinese students and faculty. Her parents had been born in Hawaii, but she grew up in Shanghai. She was in the United States studying English at Wellesley College. They were married on July 10, 1949, and had three children: Frederick, Courtney, and Juliette. The Wangs became naturalized American citizens in April 1955.

Invents major advance for computers

Wang was introduced by E. Leon Chaffee (1885–1975), who supervised his doctoral thesis at Harvard, to Howard Aiken (1900–1973), a pioneer of modern computing who ran the Harvard Computation Laboratory. Aiken and his team of scientists had created one of the first computers. Called the Mark I, the computer filled an entire room because it relied on a mechanical process for storing and retrieving data. Aiken offered Wang a position on a team that was designing a new generation of computers. In 1948, he gave Wang the critical assignment of inventing a way to make it possible to read and record information on magnetic tape, which increased the amount of data that could be stored and also make the data much easier and faster to retrieve. There was a problem, though: In the process of retrieving and reading information from magnetic tape, the information was being destroyed.

Within three weeks, and while walking across Harvard Yard, Wang had a flash of insight: The data could be automatically rewritten in magnetic cores immediately after it was called up for reading. As he noted in *Lessons,* his 1986 autobiography, "I realized in that moment that it did not matter whether or not I destroyed the information while reading it. With the information I gained from reading the magnetic memory, I could simply rewrite [save] the data immediately afterward." Wang's method soon became a standard in computers until magnetic-core memory was replaced in the late 1960s by silicon chips, which were smaller but could store more information and retrieve it more quickly.

Wang's magnetic cores were improved in 1949 by Jay W. Forrester (1918–) at the Massachusetts Institute of Technology. Forrester organized the cores into a grid and devised ways to access information more quickly. Magnetic cores formed the basis of the early mainframe computers made by International Business Machines (IBM). These magnetic-core computers soon made IBM one of the world's largest companies. Although magnetic cores are no longer in use, they were a major improvement that led to further innovations. Computer technicians still refer to the transfer of computer memory as a "core dump."

Wang made a bold move by patenting his invention. In June 1951, he founded Wang Laboratories to develop, produce, and market applications using his memory cores and other inventions. He had about $600 in savings when he began his own business, but in his first year he earned more than he had made at Harvard the previous year. The company earned more money in each quarter for the next thirty years.

As Wang's company grew from a one-man operation to a large company, he fought a legal challenge by IBM to his patent for the memory core. The case dragged on for five years, and IBM was planning a further challenge when Wang sold his memory core patent to IBM for $400,000 in 1956. The money allowed him to expand his business and made him a wealthy man, but Wang always believed that IBM had used its tremendous resources to overpower him.

Wang's company grew steadily, selling memory cores, designing commercial uses for them, and taking on special projects with other companies. During the 1960s, the company became a pioneer in the manufacture of desktop electronic calculators. Scientists, engineers, and others in need of equipment to help them calculate traditionally used slide rules, or large mainframe computers. Wang's desktop calculator, introduced in 1965, was faster, more advanced, and more practical. It was expensive at $6,500, but much cheaper than a mainframe computer. A smaller, cheaper model sold for less than $2,000. By 1967, Wang Laboratories was posting sales of more than $1 million and employed about four hundred people.

Always a visionary, Wang changed focus in the late 1960s from calculators to word processing machines, or typewriters with electronic memories. It was a crucial decision because in 1971 the pocket calculator was manufactured by Bowmar Instruments, and calculators quickly became smaller and far less expensive than those Wang had developed just a few years earlier.

An Wang in front of a Wang computer in 1979.
© *Bettmann/Corbis.*

Wang Laboratories began producing its first word processor, the Wang 1200, in 1972. It stored data on a tape cassette, but had no means for displaying text. A major breakthrough occurred in 1976 when Wang demonstrated the first cathode ray tube (CRT)–based word processor, which allowed the typist to proofread and correct a document before printing a final copy. These early word processors greatly improved productivity in business offices. New versions were rapidly introduced that displayed the entire text of a document on a large screen and provided users with a series of menus to edit and correct their documents. The user-friendliness of Wang equipment, which took into account that new technology can be intimidating, became a hallmark of the company.

The word processor, forerunner to today's desktop and laptop computers, was a sensation, and Wang Laboratories was the major producer and distributor. Beginning in 1973, the company's earnings improved by 40 percent each year until 1983.

Lasting contributions

In 1983, Wang's holdings were estimated to be $2.3 billion, and Wang had became one of the largest and most visible philanthropists, or donors of money for a good cause, in the Boston area. He contributed to Massachusetts General Hospital, built a factory at the cost of $15 million in Boston's Chinatown district that created three hundred jobs, and donated $4 million to restore Boston's performing arts theater, which was renamed the Wang Center for the Performing Arts. He gave $6 million to create the Wang Institute of Graduate Studies for software engineers and China scholars, and contributed $4 million to Harvard University and $1 million to Wellesley College, among many other acts of philanthropy.

Beginning in 1983, however, when Wang was sixty-three years old, his company took a downturn. The marketplace was changing rapidly, as desktop computers were quickly making word processors obsolete, and just as quickly, computers became more advanced and common in work and home environments. His attempts to keep company control within the family led key executives to quit at a time of rapid change in the computer industry. The company was ill-prepared to adapt its business systems to communicate with other operating systems and was attempting to catch up with new competitors at a time when those competitors were regularly introducing new advances.

After having enjoyed a long run of success, Wang was spending the last months of his life in 1989 and 1990 trying to avoid bankruptcy. Wang died of cancer of the esophagus on March 24, 1990, and was buried in Lincoln, Massachusetts. Two years later, Wang Laboratories went bankrupt, emerged as a smaller company in 1993, and in 1997 was acquired by Eastman Kodak.

Wang's legacy remains—from contributing major advances in the evolution of the computer to an early and lasting emphasis on user-friendly approaches to technology that set the standard for all computer manufacturers. In 1986, he received the Congressional Medal of Freedom for his many accomplishments. He was the recipient of over a dozen honorary doctorates, and, among other honors, was a fellow of the American Academy of Arts and Sciences.

—*Roger Matuz*

For More Information

Books

Greene, Carol, and Jim Hargrove. *Dr. An Wang: Computer Pioneer.* New York: Children's Press, 1993.

Kenney, Charles. *Riding the Runaway Horse: The Rise and Decline of Wang Laboratories.* Boston: Little Brown & Company, 1992.

Marvis, Barbara J. *Contemporary American Success Stories: Famous People of Asian Ancestry.* Hockessin, DE: Mitchell Lane Publishers, 1995.

Wang, An, with Eugene Linden. *Lessons: An Autobiography.* Boston: Pearson Addison Wesley, 1986.

Periodicals

Hevesi, Dennis. "An Wang, 70, Is Dead of Cancer; Inventor and Maker of Computers." *New York Times* (March 25, 1990): p. 38.

Louis, Arthur M. "Doctor Wang's Toughest Case." *Fortune* (February 3, 1986): pp. 106–9.

Web Sites

Redin, James. "The Doctor and His Calculators." *X-Number: World of Calculators.* http://www.dotpoint.com/xnumber/anwang.htm (accessed on March 26, 2004).

Elie Wiesel

Born September 30, 1928
Sighet, Romania

Writer, teacher, and human rights activist

E lie Wiesel (pronounced ELL-ee vee-ZEL) is one of the world's best-known human rights activists. Wiesel is a survivor of the Nazi death camps—concentration camps run by the Nazis, a German political party which, under the direction of Adolf Hitler (1889–1945), seized control of Germany in 1933 and was responsible for the destruction of millions of European Jews, Gypsies, homosexuals, and other minorities. In the 1940s, Wiesel used his experiences to write more than forty books dealing with topics such as peace, evil versus good, and human nature. In 1978, Wiesel was appointed chairman of the President's Commission on the Holocaust (the systematic murder of more than six million European Jews by the Nazis before and during World War II [1939–45]), and in 1986 he established the Elie Wiesel Foundation for Humanity. Wiesel remains an outspoken activist whose life is dedicated to educating people on the injustices of racism so that the horrors of the Holocaust will never be repeated.

Early religious upbringing

Eliezer Wiesel was born on September 30, 1928, in the town of Sighet, Hungary (now known as Romania). He spent

"Sometimes we must interfere. When human lives are endangered, when human dignity is in jeopardy, national borders and sensitivities become irrelevant. Whenever men or women are persecuted because of their race, religion, or political views, that place must— at that moment— become the center of the universe."

Elie Wiesel. *Getty Images.*

Nazi Germany at the Start of World War II

Adolf Hitler was a soldier in the German army whose every motivation had its roots in anti-Semitism, or hatred of the Jews. In 1919, Hitler attended a meeting of the German Worker's Party, an anti-Semitic, extremist political party. He joined the party and quickly took on the responsibility of writing and distributing propaganda, or media that supports particular ideas and practices, that routinely blamed the Jews for any and all problems Germany was facing. In 1920, the party changed its name to the National Socialist German Workers' Party, or the Nazi Party.

Before long, Hitler gained power as the leader of the Nazi Party, and soon Germany came under its rule. Under Hitler's command, the "Gestapo," or secret police force, were allowed to arrest citizens for anything "suspicious," whether real or imagined. They had three minutes to pack their bags and say goodbye to friends and family; then they were taken to prison. Those arrested were Jews, homosexuals, Gypsies, and other minority populations.

Although life had been becoming increasingly difficult for Jews as Hitler rose to power, it was a living nightmare beginning in 1933, when he became dictator. Jews with money and connections could safely leave Germany, but most remained in a homeland where persecution and brutality were the norm. Nazis forbid Germans to shop or dine in Jewish establishments. By 1934, all Jews were required to wear a yellow Star of David on their clothing, and Jewish store owners had to post the star in their windows. All of this was Hitler's way of forcing the Jews into bankruptcy in an attempt to make them leave.

This attitude spread through all of society. Jews could sit only on seats designated for them on public transportation; children were taught anti-Semitic ideas and concepts in school; teachers openly criticized and ridiculed Jewish students. In 1935, the Nuremburg Laws were passed, forbidding Jews to marry non-Jews and taking away their rights as German citizens.

On November 10, 1938, Hitler ordered the violent "Night of the Broken Glass." More than ten thousand Jewish shops were looted and destroyed. Homes and synagogues, or Jewish houses of worship, were burned to the ground while fire brigades stood by and watched.

World War II began and Hitler used this opportunity to speed up his plan of ridding Germany of the "undesirables." With a focus on eastern Europe, his Nazi death squads invaded Russian towns and systematically wiped out Russian Jews. Afraid that the

his childhood in this close-knit Jewish community, raised by a religious and open-minded mother and a shopkeeper father. His father, though a firm believer in the traditional values and rituals of the Jewish faith, was considered an "emancipated" killing of innocent civilians would be too much for soldiers to handle on a regular basis, a conference was held in 1942 to determine a quicker way to get the job done. The result was what is known as the "Final Solution." Jews and other populations would be sent to concentration, or death, camps. Without delay, German engineers were forced to design buildings that could accommodate mass murder and ovens that could get rid of the proof. These camps were quickly established and remained full until remaining prisoners were liberated in 1945.

Nazis rounded up victims by arriving in town with cattle cars. In the beginning, they were told they were being "relocated" to someplace safe. They were encouraged to pack their bags. This was just a trick to get them into the boxcars. As the war progressed and word of the extermination camps spread, there was no more attempt to cover up the truth. Victims traveled in unbearable conditions with nothing to ease their discomfort and suffering. Once at the camp, they were divided into groups—families were often separated, often never to see one another again. The old, sick, and young were immediately sent to the gas chamber. The rest, after being separated by gender, were forced to perform backbreaking work.

They received little food, had minimal clothing, and were often subjected to physical and mental torture.

The camps were in competition with one another in an effort to maximize profit and death rate. Every prisoner's head was shaved, and the hair was used to stuff their mattresses. Before gassing, all jewelry and dental work was removed, to be melted and cashed in for money. Victims were forced into the gas chambers in lines, much like cattle going to slaughter. Although the prisoners believed they were merely going to shower, it quickly became obvious that they had been lied to. Through four openings in the chamber, Nazis piped in a powerful insecticide. Death came swiftly, but not without excruciating pain.

Until recently, it has been commonly accepted that approximately six million Jews died in the Holocaust. Even now, however, mass graves of murdered Russian Jews are being uncovered, so the final death toll may rise. Add to that the murdered Gypsies, homosexuals, and handicapped, and the number goes well above six million. The United States Holocaust Memorial Museum estimates that 1.5 million children perished during the Holocaust.

Jew, one who was open to, and aware of, the events of the modern-day world. He encouraged Elie to study the Talmud (writings describing traditional Jewish civil and religious laws), but also insisted that he devote some of his time to studying the modern Hebrew language as well so that he could read and understand the works of contemporary authors. Wiesel's religious intensity kept him from leading a "normal" childhood, as nearly all his time was spent studying. So devout was he that he became chronically weak from fasting, or going without food, in this case as a religious ritual.

Wiesel was particularly close to his maternal grandfather, a devoutly religious man whose influence would affect Wiesel throughout his lifetime. Life for the Wiesel family changed forever in 1943, when his Grandfather Dodye was the first member to be deported, or forcefully sent away, to the Nazi death camps in Poland. Fifteen-year-old Wiesel and his entire family, which included three sisters, suffered the same fate the following year. His mother and younger sister were gassed in the death chambers, while his father died from malnutrition and physical abuse (see box).

Wiesel was surviving at a concentration camp when he was rescued by the American Third Army in 1945. From there, he joined four hundred other Jewish orphans and was sent to France, where he spent two years in an orphanage. Because he was nearly an adult, Wiesel was given the choice to pursue religious studies or secular (nonreligious) studies. Although the horrors and evil he had witnessed during his time in the concentration camps tested his faith and belief in a loving god, he chose to continue his religious studies.

Wiesel finds his voice and makes it heard

Upon completion of his studies, Wiesel took a job as a journalist for a French newspaper. One of his assignments was to interview popular French novelist François Mauriac (1885–1970). The interview would take his life in a new direction. During their talk, Wiesel shared with Mauriac a brief account of his experiences in the death camps. Mauriac encouraged the young journalist to share his account with the world so that he could rid himself of some of the horrors he carried with him while at the same time educate humankind about the unimaginable acts of cruelty that can occur when people remain silent about injustice.

Wiesel took Mauriac's advice to heart and wrote *Night,* a memoir published in 1960 that has sold more than five million copies throughout the world and has been translated into thirty languages. During an interview for *Boldtype,* Wiesel was asked what he considers to be his best book. He replied, "Each one to me is the best. I can't choose one in particular, except for my first novel, *Night,* which is the basis for everything else. If I had not written *Night,* I would not have written anything else." The original manuscript for *Night,* written in Yiddish, was 864 pages; the author eventually reduced it to one hundred. All income from the sales of the memoir goes to a *yeshiva,* or school for Jewish studies, in Israel, which Wiesel founded in memory of his father.

The publication of *Night* brought Wiesel a degree of fame he could not have foreseen. He became the unofficial spokesman for oppressed peoples everywhere. In addition to defending the Holocaust victims, he has come to the aid of Soviet Jews; Nicaragua's Miskito Indians; Cambodian refugees; victims of famine, or hunger, in Africa; and victims of apartheid, or racial segregation, in South Africa, among others.

Becomes a U.S. citizen

Prior to the publication of his first book, Wiesel's career as a journalist demanded that he travel all over the globe. In 1956, he was sent to New York. While crossing the street, he was hit by a taxi, an accident that hospitalized him for months and confined him to a wheelchair for a year. During this time, he was unable to travel to France to renew his identity card (necessary for obtaining a U.S. visa), so he researched his options and discovered that he was eligible to become a legal resident. Five years later, he received his American passport. In 1963, he became an American citizen.

A teacher and a visionary

Wiesel has been the Andrew W. Mellow Professor in the Humanities at Boston University since 1976. In addition to teaching there, he has been the Distinguished Professor of Judaic Studies at the City University of New York and the Henry Luce Visiting Scholar in Humanities and Social Thought at Yale University. Altogether, Wiesel has acquired more than one hundred honorary degrees from learning institutions.

Elie Wiesel (middle) receives the Nobel Peace Prize on December 10, 1986. To his right is his son, Elisha, and to his left is Egil Aarvik, chairman of the Nobel committee. *AP/World Wide Photos.*

In 1978, President Jimmy Carter (1924–; served 1977–81) invited Wiesel to serve as chairman of the President's Commission on the Holocaust, a position he held until 1986. Under his supervision, the United States Holocaust Memorial Museum was established in 1980. Wiesel's vision of the museum guided its evolution, and today it is divided into areas of memorial, education, research, commemoration, and action to prevent recurrence. His primary goal was to honor the victims of the Holocaust, thereby denying the Nazis of any sense of victory. The museum stands in Washington, D.C., and is open to the public year-round, free of charge.

Wins Nobel Peace Prize

In honor of his numerous human rights achievements and efforts, and for being a person who consciously chose to live a life of good despite being a victim of evil, Wiesel was awarded the Nobel Peace Prize in 1986. Alan Dershowitz (1938–), the Felix Frankfurter Professor of Law at Harvard Law School, was among those responsible for submitting names of candidates for the award. Of Wiesel he wrote, "There are many excellent reasons for recognizing Professor Wiesel. But none is more important than his role in teaching survivors and their children how to respond in constructive peace and justice to a worldwide conspiracy of genocide, the components of which included mass killing, mass silence and mass indifference."

At the presentation ceremony, Egil Aarvik (1912–1990), chairman of the Norwegian Nobel Committee, honored Wiesel: "From the abyss of the death camps he has come as a messenger to mankind—not with a message of hate and revenge, but with one of brotherhood and atonement. He has become a powerful spokesman for the view of mankind and the unlimited humanity which is, at all times, the basis of a lasting peace. Elie Wiesel is not only the man who survived—he is also the spirit which has conquered. In him we see a man who has climbed from utter humiliation to become one of our most important spiritual leaders and guides."

Wiesel has also been awarded the Presidential Medal of Freedom, the U.S. Congressional Gold Medal, and the Medal of Liberty Award.

Establishes Foundation for Humanity

Within months of receiving the Nobel Peace Prize, Wiesel and his wife founded the Elie Wiesel Foundation for Humanity. The organization's mission is to "advance the cause of human rights by creating forums for the discussion and resolution of urgent ethical issues." The Foundation hosts conferences throughout the world, inviting artists, scientists, scholars, politicians, and even youth to gather in an effort to find humane and peaceful resolutions to the world's most pressing injustices.

—*Rebecca Valentine*

For More Information

Books

Bauer, Yehuda, and Nili Keren, eds. *A History of the Holocaust*. London: Franklin Watts, 2002.

Bitton-Jackson, Livia. *I Have Lived a Thousand Years: Growing Up in the Holocaust.* New York: Simon & Schuster Books for Young Readers, 1997.

Boas, Jacob. *We Are Witnesses: Five Diaries of Teenagers Who Died in the Holocaust.* New York: Scholastic, 1996.

Carr, Firpo W. *Germany's Black Holocaust.* Kearney, NE: Morris Pub., 2003.

Eichengreen, Lucille, and Harriet Hyman Chamberlain. *From Ashes to Life: My Memories of the Holocaust.* San Francisco: Mercury House, 1994.

Klein, Gerda Weissman. *All But My Life: A Memoir.* New York: Hill & Wang, 1995.

Perl, Lila. *Four Perfect Pebbles: A Holocaust Story.* New York: HarperTrophy, 1999.

Volavkova, Hana. *I Never Saw Another Butterfly.* New York: Schocken Books, 1994.

Wiesel, Elie. *Elie Wiesel: Conversations.* Edited by Robert Franciosi. Jackson: University Press of Mississippi, 2002.

Wiesel, Elie. *Night.* New York: Hill and Wang, 1960. Multiple reprints.

Web Sites

"Elie Wiesel: First Person Singular." *PBS.* http://www.pbs.org/eliewiesel (accessed on March 26, 2004).

The Elie Wiesel Foundation for Humanity. http://www.eliewieselfoundation.org (accessed on March 26, 2004).

"An Interview with Elie Wiesel." *Tikkun* (July-August 1999). http://www.tikkun.org/magazine/index.cfm/action/tikkun/issue/tik9907/article/990715a.html (accessed on March 26, 2004).

Lang, Anson. "Boldtype: Conversation with Elie Wiesel." *Random House.* http://www.randomhouse.com/boldtype/1299/wiesel/interview.html (accessed on March 26, 2004).

Where to Learn More

Books

Adovasio, J. M., with Jake Page. *The First Americans: In Pursuit of Archaeology's Greatest Mystery*. New York: Random House, 2002.

Barrett, Tracy. *Growing Up in Colonial America*. Brookfield, CT: Millbrook Press, 1995.

Brogan, Hugh. *The Longman History of the United States of America*. 2nd ed. London and New York: Addison Wesley Longman, 1999.

Ciongoli, A. Kenneth, and Jay Parini. *Passage to Liberty: The Story of Italian Immigration and the Rebirth of America*. New York: Regan Books, 2002.

Clark, Jayne. *The Greeks in America*. Minneapolis: Lerner Publications, 1990.

Daley, William W. *The Chinese Americans*. New York: Chelsea House, 1996.

Daniels, Roger. *Coming to America: A History of Immigration and Ethnicity in American Life*. New York: HarperCollins, 1990.

Davis, William C. *The American Frontier: Pioneers, Settlers, and Cowboys, 1800–1899*. New York: Smithmark, 1992.

Dezell, Maureen. *Irish America: Coming into Clover*. New York: Doubleday, 2000.

Dolan, Sean. *The Polish Americans*. New York: Chelsea House, 1997.

Dubofsky, Melvyn. *Industrialism and the American Worker, 1865–1920*. 3rd ed. Wheeling, IL: Harlan Davidson, 1996.

Fagan, Brian M. *Kingdoms of Gold, Kingdoms of Jade: The Americas Before Columbus.* London: Thames and Hudson, 1991.

Ferry, Steve. *Russian Americans.* Tarrytown, NY: Benchmark Books, 1996.

Fitzhugh, William W. "Puffins, Ringed Pins, and Runestones: The Viking Passage to America." In *Vikings: The North Atlantic Saga.* Edited by William W. Fitzhugh and Elisabeth I. Ward. Washington and London: Smithsonian Institution Press in association with National Museum of Natural History, 2000.

Fixico, Donald L. *Termination and Relocation: Federal Indian Policy, 1945–1966.* Albuquerque: University of New Mexico Press, 1986.

Freedman, Russell. *In the Days of the Vaqueros: The First True Cowboys.* New York: Clarion Books, 2001.

Frost, Helen. *German Immigrants, 1820–1920.* Mankato, MN: Blue Earth Books, 2002.

Gernand, Renée. *The Cuban Americans.* New York: Chelsea House, 1996.

Gonzalez, Juan. *Harvest of Empire: A History of Latinos in America.* New York: Viking, 2000.

Grossman, James R. *Land of Hope: Chicago, Black Southerners, and the Great Migration.* Chicago: University of Chicago Press, 1989.

Hawke, David Freeman. *Everyday Life in Early America.* New York: Harper & Row, 1988.

Hertzberg, Arthur. *The Jews in America: Four Centuries of an Uneasy Encounter.* New York: Simon and Schuster, 1989.

Hoobler, Dorothy, and Thomas Hoobler. *The Chinese American Family Album.* New York: Oxford University Press, 1994.

Hoobler, Dorothy, and Thomas Hoobler. *The German American Family Album.* New York and Oxford: Oxford University Press, 1996.

Hoobler, Dorothy, and Thomas Hoobler. *The Scandinavian American Family Album.* New York and Oxford: Oxford University Press, 1997.

Howe, Irving. *World of Our Fathers: The Journey of the East European Jews to America and the Life They Found and Made.* New York: Simon and Schuster, 1976.

The Irish in America. Coffey, Michael, ed., with text by Terry Golway. New York: Hyperion, 1997.

Jackson, Robert H., and Edward Castillo. *Indians, Franciscans, and Spanish Colonization: The Impact of the Mission System on California Indians.* Albuquerque: University of New Mexico Press, 1995.

Johnson, Paul. *A History of the Jews.* New York: Harper & Row, 1987.

Kitano, Harry. *The Japanese Americans.* New York: Chelsea House, 1996.

Kitano, Harry H. L., and Roger Daniels. *Asian Americans: Emerging Minorities.* Englewood Cliffs, NJ: Prentice Hall, 1995.

Kraut, Alan M. *The Immigrant in American Society, 1880–1921.* 2nd ed. Wheeling, IL: Harlan Davidson, 2001.

Lavender, David Sievert. *The Rockies*. Rev. ed. New York: HarperCollins, 1975.

Lee, Lauren. *Japanese Americans*. Tarrytown, NY: Marshall Cavendish, 1996.

Lehrer, Brian. *The Korean Americans*. New York: Chelsea House, 1996.

Loewen, James W. *Lies My Teacher Told Me: Everything Your American History Textbook Got Wrong*. New York: Touchstone Books, 1996.

Magocsi, Paul R. *The Russian Americans*. New York: Chelsea House, 1996.

McLynn, Frank. *Wagons West: The Epic Story of America's Overland Trails*. New York: Grove Press, 2002.

Middleton, Richard. *Colonial America: A History, 1565–1776*. 3rd ed. Oxford, UK: Blackwell, 2002.

Monos, Dimitris. *The Greek Americans*. New York: Chelsea House, 1996.

Nabokov, Peter, ed. *Native American Testimony*. New York: Thomas Crowell, 1978.

Odess, Daniel, Stephen Loring, and William W. Fitzhugh. "Skraeling: First Peoples of Helluland, Markland, and Vinland." In *Vikings: The North Atlantic Saga*. Edited by William W. Fitzhugh and Elisabeth I. Ward. Washington and London: Smithsonian Institution Press in association with National Museum of Natural History, 2000.

Olson, Kay Melchisedech. *Norwegian, Swedish, and Danish Immigrants, 1820–1920*. Mankato, MN: Blue Earth Books, 2002.

Palmer, Colin A. *The First Passage: Blacks in the Americas, 1502–1617*. New York: Oxford University Press, 1995.

Petrini, Catherine. *The Italian Americans*. San Diego: Lucent Books, 2002.

Phillips, David, and Steven Ferry. *Greek Americans*. Tarrytown, NY: Benchmark Books, 1996.

Piersen, William D. *From Africa to America: African American History from the Colonial Era to the Early Republic, 1526–1790*. New York: Twayne, 1996.

Pitt, Leonard. *The Decline of the Californios: A Social History of the Spanish-Speaking Californians, 1846–1890*. Berkeley: University of California Press, 1966.

Portes, Alejandro, and Rubén G. Rumbaut. *Immigrant America: A Portrait*. 2nd ed. Berkeley: University of California Press, 1996.

Press, Petra. *Puerto Ricans*. Tarrytown, NY: Benchmark Books, 1996.

Schmidley, A. Dianne. *U.S. Census Bureau, Current Population Reports, Series P23-206, "Profile of the Foreign-Born Population in the United States": 2000*. Washington, DC: U.S. Government Printing Office, 2001.

Scott, John Anthony. *Settlers on the Eastern Shore: The British Colonies in North America, 1607–1750*. New York: Facts on File, 1991.

Shannon, William. *The American Irish*. Amherst: University of Massachusetts Press, 1990.

Stegner, Page. *Winning the Wild West: The Epic Saga of the American Frontier, 1800–1899.* New York: The Free Press, 2002.

Suro, Roberto. *Strangers Among Us: How Latino Immigration Is Transforming America.* New York: Knopf, 1998.

Takaki, Ronald. *Strangers from a Different Shore: A History of Asian Americans.* Boston: Little, Brown, and Company, 1989.

Tonelli, Bill, ed. *The Italian American Reader: A Collection of Outstanding Fiction, Memoirs, Journalism, Essays, and Poetry.* New York: William Morrow, 2003.

Wepman, Dennis. *Immigration: From the Founding of Virginia to the Closing of Ellis Island.* New York: Facts on File, 2002.

Williams, Jean Kinney. *The Mormons: The American Religious Experience.* New York: Franklin Watts, 1996.

Wood, Peter H. *Strange New Land: African Americans, 1617–1776.* New York: Oxford University Press, 1996.

Periodicals

Hogan, Roseann Reinemuth. "Examining the Transatlantic Voyage." Parts I and II. *Ancestry Magazine* (Part 1: November/December 2000): vol. 18, no. 6; (Part II: March/April 2001): vol. 19, no. 2. These articles can be found online at http://www.ancestry.com/library/view/ancmag/3365.asp and http://www.ancestry.com/library/view/ancmag/4130.asp (accessed on April 1, 2004).

Peck, Ira. "How Three Groups Overcame Prejudice." *Scholastic Update* (May 6, 1998): vol. 6, no. 17, p. 12.

Rose, Jonathan. "Organized Crime: An 'Equal-Opportunity' Employer; Every American Ethnic Group Has Had Its Fingers in Organized Crime—a Fact That the Dominance of Italian-American Crime Rings Tends to Mask." *Scholastic Update* (March 21, 1986): vol. 118, p. 12.

Web Sites

"About Jewish Culture." *MyJewishLearning.com.* http://www.myjewishlearning.com/culture/AboutJewishCulture.htm (accessed on April 1, 2004).

"Africa: One Continent, Many Worlds." *Natural History Museum of Los Angeles.* http://www.nhm.org/africa/facts/ (accessed on April 1, 2004).

"The American Presidency State of the Union Messages." *The American Presidency.* http://www.polsci.ucsb.edu/projects/presproject/idgrant/site/state.html (accessed on April 1, 2004).

"American West: Transportation." *World-Wide Web Virtual Library's History Index.* http://www.ku.edu/kansas/west/trans.htm (accessed on April 1, 2004).

"Austrian-Hungarian Immigrants." *Spartacus Educational.* http://www.spartacus.schoolnet.co.uk/USAEah.htm (accessed on April 1, 2004).

Bernard, Kara Tobin, and Shane K. Bernard. *Encyclopedia of Cajun Culture.* http://www.cajunculture.com/ (accessed on April 1, 2004).

"A Brief History of Indian Migration to America." *American Immigration Law Foundation.* http://www.ailf.org/awards/ahp_0203_essay.htm (accessed on April 1, 2004).

Chinese American Data Center. http://members.aol.com/chineseusa/00cen.htm (accessed on April 1, 2004).

"Coming to America Two Years after 9-11." *Migration Policy Institute.* http://www.ilw.com/lawyers/immigdaily/letters/2003,0911-mpi.pdf (accessed on April 1, 2004).

"French Colonization of Louisiana and Louisiana Purchase Map Collection." *Louisiana Digital Library.* http://louisdl.louislibraries.org/LMP/Pages/home.html (accessed on April 1, 2004).

Guzmán, Betsy. "The Hispanic Population: Census 2000 Brief." *U.S. Census Bureau, May 2001.* http://www.census.gov/prod/2001pubs/c2kbr01-3.pdf (accessed on April 1, 2004).

"Haitians in America." *Haiti and the U.S.A.: Linked by History and Community.* http://www.haiti-usa.org/modern/index.php (accessed on April 1, 2004).

"A History of Chinese Americans in California." *National Park Service.* http://www.cr.nps.gov/history/online_books/5views/5views3.htm (accessed on April 1, 2004).

Immigration: The Living Mosaic of People, Culture, and Hope. http://library.thinkquest.org/20619/index.html (accessed on April 1, 2004).

"Landmarks in Immigration History." *Digital History.* http://www.digitalhistory.uh.edu/historyonline/immigration_chron.cfm (accessed on April 1, 2004).

Le, C. N. "The Model Minority Image." *Asian Nation: The Landscape of Asian America.* http://www.asian-nation.org/model-minority.shtml (accessed on April 1, 2004).

Logan, John R., and Glenn Deane. "Black Diversity in Metropolitan America." *Lewis Mumford Center for Comparative Urban and Regional Research, University at Albany.* http://mumford1.dyndns.org/cen2000/BlackWhite/BlackDiversityReport/black-diversity01.htm (accessed on April 1, 2004).

Lovgren, Stefan. "Who Were the First Americans?" *NationalGeographic.com.* http://news.nationalgeographic.com/news/2003/09/0903_030903_bajaskull.html (accessed on April 1, 2004).

Mosley-Dozier, Bernette A. "Double Minority: Haitians in America." *Yale–New Haven Teachers Institute.* http://www.yale.edu/ynhti/curriculum/units/1989/1/89.01.08.x.html (accessed on April 1, 2004).

RapidImmigration.com. http://www.rapidimmigration.com/usa/1_eng_immigration_history.html (accessed on April 1, 2004).

The Scottish History Pages. http://www.scotshistoryonline.co.uk/scothist.html (accessed on April 1, 2004).

Simkin, John. "Immigration." *Spartacus Educational.* http://www.spartacus.schoolnet.co.uk/USAimmigration.htm (accessed on April 1, 2004).

Spiegel, Taru. "The Finns in America." *Library of Congress: European Reading Room.* http://www.loc.gov/rr/european/FinnsAmer/finchro.html (accessed on April 1, 2004).

"The Story of Africa: Slavery." *BBC News.* http://www.bbc.co.uk/world service/africa/features/storyofafrica/9chapter9.shtml (accessed on April 1, 2004).

Trinklein, Mike, and Steve Boettcher. *The Oregon Trail.* http://www.isu.edu/%7Etrinmich/Oregontrail.html (accessed on April 1, 2004).

"U.S. Immigration." *Internet Modern History Sourcebook.* http://www.fordham.edu/halsall/mod/modsbook28.html (accessed on April 1, 2004).

Virtual Museum of New France. http://www.civilization.ca/vmnf/vmnfe.asp (accessed on April 1, 2004).

Index

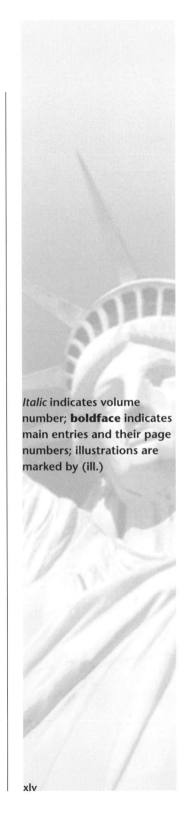

F

Factory workers, child, *1:* 216
Farm workers
   Chávez, César, and, *1:* 84–85, 87–92
   Hernández, Antonia, and, *1:* 169
Fasting, *1:* 89–90
Fathers, immigrant, *1:* 6
Fermi, Enrico, *1:* 118 (ill.), **118–25**
Fermi-Dirac statistics, *1:* 119
Fermions, *1:* 119
Figley, Charles, *1:* 101
Filipinos. *See* Philippines
Fillmore, Millard, *1:* 126 (ill.), **126–33,** 130 (ill.), 131 (ill.)
Films. *See* Movies
Final Solution, *2:* 405. *See also* Holocaust
Fishes, fossil, *1:* 11–12
Fishes of Brazil (Agassiz), *1:* 11
Fiske, Nathan, *1:* 194–95
Fluxus movement, *2:* 275
Fly (Ono), *2:* 277
Football, *2:* 304, 305–11
Ford, Gerald, *1:* 60; *2:* 229, 233
Forest Hills Diary (Cuomo), *1:* 105
Forrester, Jay W., *2:* 398–99
Fort Astoria, *1:* 37, 37 (ill.)
Fossil fishes, *1:* 11–12
Four Horsemen, *2:* 309
442nd Regimental Combat Team, *1:* 185–88; *2:* 238
The Four Winners (Rockne), *2:* 310
Fourth World Conference on Women, *1:* 22
Fragrant Hill Hotel, *2:* 286
France
   French Revolution, *2:* 293, 366–67, 382–83
   Great Debate, *2:* 383
   Statue of Liberty and, *2:* 363–64, 368
   Third Republic of, *2:* 364
Frankenstein, 2: 255
Frankfurter, Felix, *1:* 134 (ill.), **134–42,** 140 (ill.)
Franklin, Benjamin, *2:* 289, 291
Fred Karno Company, *1:* 78
Freed slaves, *2:* 391
Freedom of religion. *See* Religious freedom

Freedom of speech, *1:* 138
Freedom Rides, *2:* 239
Frémont, John, *1:* 131 (ill.)
French Revolution
   Delacroix, Eugene, and, *2:* 366–67
   English Dissenters and, *2:* 293
   Tocqueville, Alexis de, and, *2:* 382–83
Frias, Miguel, *1:* 27
Frick, Henry Clay, *1:* 72
Fricke, David, *2:* 279
Fugitive Slave Act, *1:* 129–30; *2:* 391
Fur trade, *1:* 33, 34–38, 35 (ill.), 37 (ill.)

G

Galbraith, Erle, *1:* 208–9
Galleon Award, *2:* 270
Garvey, Marcus, *1:* 143 (ill.), **143–51**
Gays, *2:* 404
Gaza Strip, *2:* 330, 332
General relativity, *1:* 115
German immigrants
   1830, after, *2:* 384
   1840s–50s, *2:* 244
   national identity of, *2:* 263–64
Gershwin, George, *1:* 206, 208
Gestapo, *2:* 404
Giants in the Earth (Rölvaag), *2:* 325–26
Gipp, George, *2:* 307–9
The Gipper, *2:* 308–9
"Give Peace a Chance" (Lennon), *2:* 277
Glaciers, *1:* 10, 14–16, 15 (ill.)
Glazer, Nathan, *2:* 259, 263–64
Global Village Foundation, *1:* 166
"God Bless America" (Berlin), *1:* 158
Goddard, Paulett, *1:* 80
Gold Rush. *See* California Gold Rush
Golden Age of Television, *2:* 377
The Golden Girls, 2: 379
Golway, Terry, *1:* 107
Gordon, William, *1:* 29–30
Gorn, Elliot, *1:* 212
Gould, Jay, *2:* 300

N

NAACP (National Association for the Advancement of Colored People), *1:* 148–49
NAFTA (North American Free Trade Agreement), *1:* 96
Nagasaki, Japan, *1:* 123 (ill.), 124
Nakahara, Mary. *See* Kochiyama, Yuri
Napoleon. *See* Bonaparte, Louis-Napoléon
NASA (National Aeronautics and Space Administration), *1:* 96
Nation of Islam, *2:* 237
National Academy of Sciences, *1:* 16
National Aeronautics and Space Administration (NASA), *1:* 96
National Association for the Advancement of Colored People (NAACP), *1:* 148–49
National Audubon Society, *1:* 48
National Center for Atmospheric Research, *2:* 283
National Defense Research Committee, *2:* 283
National Farm Workers Association, *1:* 88
National Gallery of Art (Washington D.C.), *2:* 284 (ill.), 284–85
National identity, *2:* 263–64
National Islam, *1:* 149
National Organization of Women (NOW), *2:* 272
National Socialist Party (Nazi). *See also* Hitler, Adolf; Holocaust
concentration camps, *2:* 403, 405, 406–7
Einstein, Albert, and, *1:* 116, 117
Fermi, Enrico, and, *1:* 120
Kissinger, Henry, and, *2:* 230
rise of, *2:* 404
World War II and, *2:* 404–5
Native Americans
alcoholic beverages and, *1:* 39
epidemics and, *1:* 221
fur trade and, *1:* 35 (ill.), 38
Jackson, Helen Hunt, and, *1:* 194, 198–99
miners and, *1:* 197
relocation of, *1:* 197–98

Tocqueville, Alexis de, on, *2:* 386
trappers and, *1:* 197
wagon trains and, *1:* 221
Western Movement and, *1:* 196–97
NATO. *See* North Atlantic Treaty Organization (NATO)
Natori Company, *2:* 267, 268–71
Natori, Josie, *2:* 267 (ill.), **267–72**
Natori, Kenneth, *2:* 268, 270
Natural history, *1:* 11–16
Natural selection, *1:* 13, 14
Nazi party. *See* National Socialist Party (Nazi)
Negro Factories Corporation, *1:* 147
The Negro World, *1:* 146
"The New Colossus" (Lazarus), *2:* 243, 247–48, 248 (ill.), 370, 372–73
New England immigrants, *2:* 387
New Hampshire and Catholic immigrants, *1:* 128
The New Republican, *1:* 136–37
New York City
immigrant population, *2:* 259, 263–64
Moynihan, Daniel Patrick, and, *2:* 261–62
New York Manufacturing Company, *2:* 358
New York Morning Journal, *2:* 301–2
New York Public Library, *1:* 41
New York Stock Exchange 1929 collapse, *1:* 152–53
New York World, *2:* 300–302
Newspapers, *2:* 296, 299–303
Newton, Isaac, *1:* 114, 115
Nez Perce Tribe, *1:* 220–28
Nicaragua, *1:* 191
Night (Wiesel), *2:* 406–7
"Night of the Broken Glass," *2:* 404
Nimitu Tribe, *1:* 220–28
Nixon, Richard
Buchanan, Pat, and, *1:* 59–60
election of, *1:* 190
Kissinger, Henry, and, *2:* 229, 231, 234
Moynihan, Daniel Patrick, and, *2:* 263, 265
Soviet Union and, *2:* 233

260 — (set)